1001 Horror Writing Prompts

That will motivate you creatively

- -

CHRISTINA ESCAMILLA

.

INTRODUCTION

Dear Reader,

Horror is my jam. It is my lifeblood and the genre I feel most comfortable writing in. I have no idea what that says about my psyche, but I'm no stranger to scaring the metaphorical pants off of readers. So what is it about horror that is so fascinating?

In many ways, horror is just a reflection of the terrible truths in life we try our hardest to ignore. It is the stripping away of all the layers of humanity in order to take an unapologetic look at the ugliness that lies within. Sometimes this is framed by using creatures or crazed murderers, even if they come off as campy, while other times we let the fear itself be front and center.

When you write in the horror genre, don't focus on the "fear factor." You may have a creepy setting, or never-before-seen monster, and you may even have an amazing plot, but that's not the thing that's going to scare your readers. What will really scare them is when you can find the fear itself (fear of death, of being alone, of fire, etc.) and then build your story off of that.

If you can do that, then these prompts will only be used as a platform to pass that fear onto your readers, and when that happens – well, there's a good chance they may not be sleeping tonight.

Happy Haunting,

Christina

How to Use This Book

For Horror, because the sheer amount of overused tropes are abundant, you must take care to use them as integral aspects to your story, rather than for shock value. Of course, splatterpunk, shock fiction, and other pieces designed to force reader disgust is a subset of the horror genre, it is still important to have a lot of thought into what kind of themes and plot devices you thrust into your terrifying tale.

That said, there are still themes that tend to overlap naturally. For instance, a tale about a masked murderer might also slip in an underling theme of religious fanaticism. To this extent, there is no rule that says you must fit your story neatly inside of a box. With that in mind, I tried to provide a diverse collection that offer you a great deal to work with, but you will also find some overlap even in these prompts as well. Moreover, some prompts are inspired from real life history, events, and so forth.

Not only is each theme placed into parts, but rather than using open ended questions, which is common in many prompt books, I simply offered a catalyst for a story. For this reason I used words such as "unnamed character" or "protagonist" and many gender neutral terms. The key is to build YOUR story around these ideas, including your own unique characters.

Feel free to share what you've come up with. I would love to see these prompts have life!

Table of Contents

Demons, Occult, & Paranormal Themes

Fears, Paranoia, & Psychological Undertones

Monsters, Creatures, & Creepy Crawlies

Demons, Occult, & Paranormal Themes

One of the most popular subgenres in horror is supernatural fiction. Although we will deal with paranormal beings specifically in a later section, the inclusion of supernatural elements in horror seems to be making a resurgence lately. As intelligent beings, we have an inherent need to explore the world around us. To make sense of what we cannot explain. As such, too often we create myths, legends, and other scenarios in order to give ourselves some stewardship over reality. At times, this can swing wildly out of control and when it does, it can be downright terrifying. From the depths of illusions of our own making come religious fervor, cults, and the unexplained.

Cults

Drawing from real-life horror, the very nature of cults are basked in the paranormal simply because of their religious connotations. The point of a cult is to take the accepted view of religion, which is entirely based on individual perception, and then elevate it to the extreme. It is the kind of religious fanaticism that creates the Branch Davidians, People's Temple, Heaven's Gate, and other real-life cults that have existed with many horrific consequences. When cults are used as a horror trope, it doesn't just take from the darker realities of the need for acceptance and the hivemind, but it often mirrors them.

1. When pamphlets bearing an invitation to *The Brotherhood of the Forgotten One* meeting is posted around campus, a group of unnamed characters think

nothing of it. They assume it's most likely some new, and probably lame, Greek organization that is starting up, but with the promise of free beer who can say no? They show up to the meeting and discover they are kind of right. It *is* a Greek organization, but aside from hazing, drinking, and other outlets associated with Greek life, the brotherhood also needs a few willing sacrifices for their god.

2. An unnamed character is on a giant slab, about to be sacrificed in front of a dozen or so cult members. When their hoods are pulled back the character only sees familiar faces.

3. During a heavy rainstorm, an unnamed character hears the sound of distant shouting. They try to ignore it, but when the screams escalate the character finally picks up the phone to call the police. Unfortunately, the line is dead. Braving the weather they go out themselves, only to find a group of people being held under the water in the nearby riverbank. Their captives are wearing animal masks and screaming, "Cleanse thine soul from worldly pleasures!"

4. When an unnamed character's roommate starts to act a little odd, it's easy to blame it on their recent break up. However, it isn't long before the roommate starts to dress

in strange outfits and refers to the character as a "false friend." By this time they are considering moving, but they never get that chance. One day they wake up and find their roommate has already beaten them to the punch. The character is relieved, but they shouldn't be. The roommate is about to be replaced by a member of the same cult. This one is much, much worse.

5.   An unnamed character arrives in a small town hoping that they have finally found somewhere to settle down with their family. The neighbors are all friendly and stand out because of how attractive they all look. In fact, many of them look like they just stepped off a photoshoot. The new family's life falls into routine, but something strange begins to happen – one by one who they are begins to chip away, from their physical appearance to their overall compliance towards the town's mayor.

6.   Every morning at exactly 6am, an unnamed character begins to notice their neighbor has taken to going outside and kneeling three times in front of a mound of dirt. It's an odd habit, but who are they to pry? Then another begins the strange ritual, followed by another and another. Finally, the unnamed character has had enough and crosses into the yard, trampling over the dirt in the process. That's when their once quiet neighbors begin to scream, running towards them with vacant eyes.

7. "Everything you know is a lie." It's the first words said to an unnamed character as they sit strapped to a strong metal chair. As soon as the phrase is uttered they cry out in pain while electric sparks whiz through their body. The electricity removes and defragments bits of memory, faces of loved ones, and indeed; everything they have ever learned. When it's all over the only thing left is the face of the Great One, the old one, and the only thing that now matters.

8. The idea that the world is going to end is a concept that factors into a lot of cults. Many times, this is outside the scope of cultist control. Not this group. When the world doesn't end on the date they predict, they are just going to have to make it so.

9. During the demolition of an old dilapidated building, a thousand mournful cries can be heard from somewhere underneath the ground. Startled, the workers go to investigate only to find a tunnel system built directly underneath the now open floorboards. Inside the tunnel a group of pale-faced people are discovered, their eyes are glossy and weak from lack of use. What's worse is that these people start screaming and attacking the workers at once, claiming that their sacred grounds have now been ruined.

10. A group of recent grads are taking a road trip to celebrate their new adult life. On the way to their destination, they stop at a local gas station. The attendees are all wearing the same military garb, complete with an axe insignia. The attendees are very convincing that the grads are in a warzone and they are a type of secret military police. By the time the grads realize it's nothing more than an overzealous cult, it's too late; half of them are already members.

11. After leaving a cult, a former member simply wants to get on with their life and start over again. Perhaps one day this may be possible, but for now, every time the character leaves their house there seems to be strangers across the way, staring at them with binoculars. They don't exactly look too friendly either.

12. For years, an unnamed character has been trying to get a loved one out of a cult. Nothing they do seems to work. Then one night, after trying once more to convince them to leave to no avail, the character has an epiphany. The only way to save their loved one is to kill them all.

13. After escaping from a cult an unnamed character continues to have horrific dreams about the dreadful time they spent among what they now deem "the crazies."

What plagues them the most is that there are others still living in such an oppressive environment. Finally, the character decides that the only way the dreams will stop is if they go back and try to face their fears by helping the others. When they return, the "crazies" are all waiting for them, with no intentions of getting out.

14. An unnamed character has an addition to a new street drug called Zirdoxx. It consumes every moment of their waking time. To get clean, and get their life back on track, the character joins a drug treatment program that promises to fix "all life's ills" as shown through a local ad in the paper. Their methods are weird, really weird, but effective. It isn't until the character is clean, however, that they realize they have inadvertently joined a cult.

15. As a form of mind control, members of this strange group are only given numbers instead of names. After years of being called Member 17645, an unnamed character discovers some hidden files and finally remembers their true name. After having their identity restored, the character realizes how much they've missed being a whole person. The goal is now to get out, but in order to do so they're going to have to get past Member 1 through 17644.

16. At the checkout counter, an unnamed character attempts to pay, but is quickly told by the cashier that the "All

Father" has already covered what is owed. Thanking their good fortune the character quickly takes their purchases and leaves. When they return back to the store, during another shopping trip, the cashier is nowhere in sight and they are back to paying full price for their groceries. A few days later, however, the cashier shows up at the character's door and demands repayment.

17. Deep within the woods, a group worships the mother of the trees. The locals know of this cult, but because they are passive and do no harm, the townspeople leave them alone. When the great mother awakens though, all of that changes.

18. One scandalous news story occurred in the 1980s, when a group of day care workers were accused of running a Satanic cult. Although there were additional allegations regarding abuse of the children, suppose only the former part is true. Sort of. Perhaps, these poor souls really are innocent, but there *is* a Satanic cult at the facility. Orchestrated by the children themselves.

19. The unnamed character was going to defend their house against the "freaks" if it was the last thing they did. The people in question had been buying up the property on this street for the last six months and the character is the last holdout. They are convinced that each house that is

bought is used for horrific rituals conducted by the strange group, and they want no part of it. Then one day the unnamed character gets an offer they can't refuse, but it isn't exactly money they're accepting.

20. Every dog that entered Snuffy Doo's Poodle Parlor came out looking rather bizarre. Not bad just...*odd*. All of these poor critters returned to their masters with lion tails, mohawks, and other strange cuts that weren't originally requested. It's relatively harmless, but annoying. That is until the pets start attacking their owners.

21. Some say a group of wild children haunt the underground sewers in the city. Others say the idea is ludicrous and chalk the strange sightings to be nothing more than someone's overactive imagination. A documentary filmmaker is determined to find out which is true and so the unnamed character heads down into the depths with their trusty camera. Once there, the filmmaker doesn't find the children, but fully grown adults with ill-fitting clothes. Strangely, the clothing styles would have been popular in the 1970s.

22. During an upcoming election, the local townspeople see signs that read "Zenox for Prez." There is a lot of muttering about who this Zenox person is, but that conversation begins to lessen as more and more signs

begin to show up. Before long, there is only one lawn without a sign and the unknown character who owns it is about to get a strange knock at the door.

23. On the table in front of an unnamed character is a prescription bottle in their name. "Do it," The voice on the intercom barks. "I don't think I can," The character mutters. "DO IT." Trembling, the character picks up a fistful of pills and proceeds.

24. A nosy neighbor has been watching the house down the lane since the strange couple moved in. It had been about four months now and the first night they seemed relatively normal. Then more and more family members, who didn't look anything alike, started to show up. Soon the neighborhood pet population also decreased drastically. The more strange things that happen, the more the neighbor feels inclined to watch. Little do they know, the group is watching back.

25. An unnamed character receives an unexpected knock at the door. When the character opens it, they are greeted to the sight of a little old lady selling black muffins out of a basket. The character wouldn't normally think anything of the scene, expect for the fact that behind the woman, at every house on the street, there are other old ladies. All dressed exactly alike. Selling muffins.

26.   The cause of death is said to be cyanide and the unnamed
        character is the lead detective who is working the case.
        The obvious conclusion is that this is a cult. But, the story
        isn't that cut and dry. This isn't the only segment of this
        cult, and soon, there will be millions if not billions dead.

27.   An unnamed character is on their very first sleepover.
        They were delighted at the invite, since they don't really
        have a lot of friends at school and as a result, they are
        willing to ignore how peculiar their friend's parents are
        acting. By morning, after a night of unexplained
        occurrences they are eager to get back home, only to find
        their friend's parents blocking the door. "But, this is your
        home now," They cry.

28.   An unnamed character prides themselves on being a
        nonconformist. They dress, act, and think differently than
        the norm. Then one day others begin to follow suit,
        emulating the unnamed character exactly. The character
        has inadvertently created a cult. Very quickly do they
        realize how easy it is to become mad with power.

29.   During a routine day at the police station, a strange figure
        decked out in a red robe enters the building and begins to
        chant in an indiscernible language. Before anyone can
        react to the sight, the robed individual takes out a knife

begins to stab themselves repeatedly. The police react quickly, but little do they know, more cult members are on their way.

30. A small time author amasses a cult following without realizing it. At first, it's just a few postings on message boards, then comes very odd individuals at book signings. Before long, the author is tormented by these "fans" that won't leave them alone.

31. An unnamed character, frustrated with how little life has offered them, joins a cult that insists the end of the world is imminent. The unnamed character has doubts, but stays because it gives their life meaning. On the night of the "Great Departure", which the character knows little about, everyone is given a glass of wine to celebrate the end of the world. It isn't until after the character takes a large swig that they realize they've just drunk poison.

32. An unnamed character desperately wants to join a cult, but is told that they must accomplish three tasks before gaining entrance. The first is to change their name and get rid of their old identity, which is easy enough. The second is to sell off all their possessions and give that, along with any other monetary funds, to the organization. This is a little harder, but is still accomplished. Then, they are told they must kill their family.

33. A cult is thinly veiled as an alternative political party. They stand for a lot of what the populace wants – clean energy, more job creation, less social issues being tackled by the government, and ritualistic sacrifice for those that oppose their ideologies.

34. A group of unnamed characters are taken in the dead of night right out of their beds. Black veils are placed over their heads and they are driven to a remote location. Once there, they are tied to a chair and the veils are removed. Little do they know, they have committed slights against this strange cult without realizing it.

35. A young, unnamed character joins an off-campus organization thinking it will give them a good alternative to college and mainstream life. Their newly chosen membership is going quite well, until they are witness to a murder that the cult commits and are then sworn to secrecy. Leaders of the group threaten that, should they tell, the character will be next.

36. An unnamed character begins to date someone they have been pining after for quite some time. A few months into the relationship and they begin to realize there's something a little odd about this person that they never noticed before. By the time they are privy to their

partner's cult status, they're already in too deep and leaving could be deadly.

Religious Fervor

This theme closely relates to the nature of cults in that it focuses on the idea of religion and what it might mean if a socially acceptable line is crossed. However, unlike the cult theme, religious fervor doesn't need to draw on the idea of sociability itself. There is no group here, but rather an internal belief held by an individual whose religion can usually only be understood by one person – themselves.

37. Asceticism is a term used to describe a lifestyle in which an individual turns away from what is commonly perceived to be worldly pleasures, such as taking joy in food, relationships, intimacy, etc. Craft a narrative in which an unnamed character believes that this ideology is the only way they can elevate themselves onto a new plane of existence. But, turning away from the sins of the world is really, *really* hard. They decide that the only way to give up societal pleasures is by destroying society altogether.

38. While inside a busy shopping center a group of teens hear shouting a few stores over followed by the sound of shots being fired. It isn't long before a strange voice comes out

over the PA system, warning everyone that the cleansings will now commence and only the chosen will remain.

39.   An unnamed character has joined a new religion that seems nothing short of a Utopia. Everyone is happy, peaceful, and all of their needs seem to be met. That's because one night a month they go out and pursue the most vile Earthly urges. Including murder.

40.   An unnamed character takes a leisurely stroll down their suburban neighborhood when a black car pulls up beside them. The window is rolled down and a stranger in an animal mask asks if them if they believe in the God of Nature. When the reply is no, the character is shot and the car drives away, moving on to their next victim.

41.   They call them the smiley ones. For months now, suicides have been taking place all over the world. Though this in itself isn't strange, how the deed is done is downright bizarre. Each body is found hanging outside the window, not with a rope around their neck, but hooks in their mouth; forcing a grimace as the flesh rips and gravity takes over. In each of their pocket is a strange manifesto from a religion that no one has heard of.

42.   An unnamed character is approached by a stranger in a trench coat. "Are you unhappy?" The stranger asks. In all

truthfulness, the stranger is not happy, and the moment they have that thought, the stranger touches them. The unnamed character suddenly has a new zest for life, believing in a higher power, and a strange innate need to kill for that belief.

43. Every five years it's the eve of blood, a time in which a sacrifice must be made in order to appease the gods. Little does an unnamed character know, they are the chosen victim, as ordained in the great prophecy.

44. A disease riddled character finds solace inside a hospice, knowing that soon their suffering will be over. However, one day another patient runs into their room, cured from head to toe. Eagerly, they begin to convert the character to their newfound faith – believe and you can receive full health. The only cost is one's soul.

45. A young unnamed character is forced to spend the summer at their grandparent's house each year. They are allowed to explore every room in the estate but the attic. This year they are determined to sneak in. When they do, they find a strange alter, complete with candles, incense...and human remains.

46. "Our father who art in heaven, hallowed be thy name. Thy kingdom..." The words are repeated over and over again

by a mental patient inside an asylum. Generally, the guards ignore them, but this time the patient breaks their mantra to let out one chilling phrase, "It's time. He's here."

47.   It begins with a throbbing pain inside an unnamed character's head. Then it escalates to murmurings before they are tormented by the sound of a booming voice, commanding them to do all sorts of strange tasks. The character can't quite understand if they are going mad or if this is truly the voice of God.

48.   The unnamed character is sick, very sick. Blood trickles down the front of their lips, splashing all over their favorite shirt and their skin is pallor stricken. They chalk it up to one very bad cold, but it isn't a cold. It is the beginning of a curse, and it will only get worse.

49.   The ritual is almost complete, but the unnamed character can't seem to perform the final task. They have the fire, and they have their sacred robes of cleansing, but they just can't bring themselves to perform the last act – walk into the flames.

50.   A local police station receives a series of cryptic messages that are strangely signed with an upside down cross. The

officers are willing to pass the whole thing off as a hoax; that is, until body parts begin to show up.

51. An unnamed character finds themselves locked in a small room, wearing the skull of a large animal. The more they struggle, the tighter the skull becomes. In the recesses of the darkness they can hear chanting and before long, dozens of robed figures begin to kneel in front of them. They can't quite figure out if they're are being worshipped, or about to be sacrificed.

52. One day an unnamed character finds their child has come home from school and is rather detached – not even a hello, just straight to their room. Over the course of the next few months, the child becomes more and more withdrawn. Then the truth is found out, a new religion is to blame, and the consequences of joining are deadly.

53. Total control. That's what one has to give up in order to become one with the godly entity. But, what does that mean? One unnamed character is about to find out.

54. While getting lost in the backroads, an unnamed character finds an old, dilapidated house. They are apprehensive, but still hopeful the owner might have a phone that they can borrow. After knocking, a strange man answers and then begins to scream. As it turns out,

they were under the impression that the apocalypse, brought down by an angry god, has happened and are surprised to see the face of another survivor.

55. An unnamed character has been out drinking when they stumble into a darkened alleyway. There they find a stranger covered in odd tattoos, from head to foot. Without warning, the stranger grabs the character and begins to drag them into a nearby sewer. "I'm sorry." They murmur, "God has commanded it."

56. An unnamed character has been arguing with a roommate for quite some time. Normally, the two would just yell at each other or leave little passive aggressive notes. This time, the roommate is silent. Eerily so. Within a week the roommate shaves their head and stops sleeping. One day the character finds a religious pamphlet that outlines how to go about "letting go of the mortal world."

57. Imagine the above scenario, but rather than finding a pamphlet that will outline some horrible act of self-destruction for the roommate, the character finds a book full of past and future sacrificial victims. There's also a picture of themselves, with a red circle around the photo.

58. When an unnamed character moves into a small town, they are warned by neighbors to stay away from the house

at the end of the lane. Of course, the character doesn't listen and late one night they sneak into the yard and peer into the open window, curiosity getting the best of them. They watch in horror as an elderly gent commits an atrocious act in the name of their religion.

59.   An unnamed character gets an unusual phone call from a relative asking for a large sum of money. Normally, they would decline, but the relative sounds so desperate that they oblige. A few days later, it happens again, and the request is larger and larger until the character demands to know what the money is being used for. The relative responds that they cannot share this with a nonbeliever. The character decides against letting them borrow any more money, and a few days later, the relative dies.

60.   An unnamed character takes a deep breath and readies the trigger. The gun is aimed at the elected official's head. They aren't sure about this mission, but they know it's the only way they'll be forgiven. Taking another deep breath, they fire.

61.   An unnamed character picks up a hitchhiker on a winding, desolate road. As soon as the car door shuts, the stranger starts talking. By the end of the car ride, the character is convinced that the day of reckoning is upon them. There's only one way out – kill all the nonbelievers.

62.   An unnamed character suffers a severe brain injury and is convinced they are a walking deity. At first, no one believes what they say, but then they begin to amass a small following. Before long, they are leading several thousands of members and if they are not careful, it will only end in death.

63.   "Living mummy" is a concept derived from the process of starving oneself in such a way that when they die, the individual will become a calcified mummy. They do this in order to reach a certain plane of enlightenment. Envision a scenario in which an unnamed character is undergoing this ritual, but begins to regret it halfway through the process. Unfortunately, it's too late to turn back now.

64.   An unnamed character is in the middle of a parade when a series of explosions ring out. From somewhere in the crowd a voice cries, "Destroy the sinners." Another few bombs go off and screams can be heard everywhere. From amongst the chaos, the character finds the voice startlingly familiar.

65.   Envision the above scenario, but instead draft the narrative from the perspective of the one behind the religious based attack. Concentrate especially on the

wayward ideologies that would cause the individual to commit such a horrible act.

66. An unnamed character is approached by a stranger who claims that the character's self-sacrifice will save the world. It's an odd request, but the stranger is so convincing. The character must decide whether to sacrifice themselves on faith alone, or decide to forgo it – potentially risking the lives of everyone they love.

67. For years, a young unnamed character has seen their friends be taken into a dark van, strapped with an odd vest before they go, never to return. One day, it's the character's turn and when they put the vest on, the adult who tends to them whispers, "Thank you for your death. The great one is pleased. Our enemies will be no more."

68. A stranger places a gun to the head of an unnamed character and pulls the trigger. The bullet goes in, but a few seconds later it slides back out and falls to the ground. "You see," the stranger says in delight. "I was right, you are the one true God."

69. A voodoo priestess wants to try a spell that will destroy her enemies, allowing her succeed financially. The spell calls for items like chicken feet, certain rare herbs, and the body of a recently deceased human being.

70. An unnamed character is an officer who gets a call about a man bathing in the river. Thinking it might be some poor homeless person, the officer responds only to be told by the man that he is "wishing away his sins." The officer asks why and very clearly the man says, "So I don't end up like them." Looking to where he is pointing, the officer sees several bodies floating in the river.

71. An unnamed character receives a notice in the mail that their relative has passed and they have been left property in the will. When arriving at their new house they are told no one has gone through the house since their relative's death. It isn't long until they stumble upon a room that is covered in red paint. On the floor is a pentagram with bone shards littered across.

72. When an unnamed character's boat capsizes they spend several days floating on the water, desperate to survive. When all seems to be lost they are visited by what they believe is an angel. Hope does not spring quickly, however, because without warning the strange being begins to pull them below the water's surface.

73. An unnamed character, who is an Atheist, finally relents to their friend's begging and decides to attend church. Once there, the priest turns the crucifix upside down and

the congregation apprehends the character. The priest then thanks them for their sacrifice.

ESP

Extrasensory Perception, the sixth sense, or ESP, as it is often called is the idea of having an inner sense of knowing beyond what is humanly capable. In some cases, individuals with this additional sense are said to be able to view objects remotely, while in other, more bizarre cases, this sense is marked by the ability to communicate with the dead. Typically, these special "abilities" will manifest in the following ways:

- **Clairaudience:** The paranormal ability to hear beyond the normal scope.
- **Clairalience:** The paranormal ability to smell beyond the normal scope.
- **Clairgustance:** The paranormal ability to taste beyond the normal scope.
- **Claircognizance:** Perhaps the most common form, this is the ability to simply have intrinsic knowledge beyond what is considered humanly possible.

Keep these specific ability groups in mind when you weave ESP traits into your characters or the plot itself.

74.   A mortuary student is finally able to deal with the deceased during an advanced pathology course. When the body is first rolled in the student jumps, assuming that one of the TAs are playing a prank by yelling. However,

no one else seems to be hearing the noises either. That's when the student realizes the noises is coming from the still-sewn lips of the deceased.

75.   While watching television a young unnamed character hears a series of voices inside their head. It comes on suddenly and they are terrified they might be going crazy. Normally, one might blame mental illness, but the voices are getting more clear and so far, everything they say will happen has come to pass.

76.   An unnamed character has the gift of knowing when others will die. So far they've used it only to score small winnings in celebrity death pools. Then one day they realize that they can use their gift to prevent the death of others. For a price.

77.   Since they are little, an unnamed character has had a recurring nightmare that they will die in a car crash on their 16th birthday. When the day nears, they finally convince themselves that there is nothing to worry about – until their parents surprise them with a brand new car.

78.   An unnamed character gets lost on their way to a city they have never been before. Their GPS system keeps glitching and they can't seem to read the map right. They take a left, when they should have taken a right, and end up in the

middle of a cemetery. At once they begin to hear murmurs, which grow louder and louder the further into the graveyard they drive. This has never happened to them before. Then again, they've never been this close to the dead before.

79. During a routine pregnancy a woman gives birth to her third child. Curiously, one of the nurses begins to act strangely. The closer to the birth it gets, the more nervous the nurse acts. Finally, when the baby's head emerges the nurse jumps back with a jolt. "I knew it! I knew it!" the nurse says before running out of the room. The other nurse quickly makes a grab for the baby, hoping to finish the process, but as soon as she lays eyes on the newborn, she screams.

80. An unnamed character spots a homeless person sitting in the park, pouring over a collection of newspapers scattered around them. Feeling sympathetic, the character stops over and offers them a few bucks for a hot meal. Curiosity getting the best of them, they inquire about the papers. "I'm looking for clues!" The homeless person cries. "They're all in here, clues about the future. Yes. Here, right here. You see? A clue about...about war." At that moment, the first bomb drops.

81.   A young babysitter gets a call from one of their favorite clients about sitting the usual children, plus one. Seeing the opportunity to make a little extra cash, the babysitter readily agrees. As soon as the parents leave, the additional child looks at the character and begins howling. After finally calming them down enough to speak, the child cries, "The bad man is going to kill you tonight."

82.   After spending years attached at the hip, two conjoined twins are finally separated and go about leading very different lives in opposite ends of the world. Each year they make plans to visit each other, but it always falls through. Then one day one twin drops dead from heart failure. Across the world, the other twin suddenly drops to the ground and begins to wail uncontrollably.

83.   One day, while having an argument with a significant other an unnamed character becomes so enraged that dishes begin to fly off the shelves without anyone touching them. As a result of the strange display, the partner leaves. The character is so distraught that they fall to the ground and sob. From somewhere on the opposite side of the house, a gun begins to slide out from inside a closed drawer.

84.   An unnamed character visiting a psychic wants to know if the person they are in love with loves them back. Without

warning the psychic goes into a trance and begins to mutter incoherently. Finally, their words come out clearer, "Yes. They love you, and they are also in grave danger."

85. Envision a scenario in which an unnamed character goes to a hypnotist in order to help control their anxiety. Under hypnosis the character begins to recall a past life, vividly remembering the horrifying way in which they died.

86. During a psychological examination to test the propensity for a patient's ESP, a series of cards are placed faced down. The patient is urged to guess what symbol is underneath each card. They guess them all correctly, showcasing their psychic ability. Once finished, the patient looks at the examiner and says plainly, "I know what you did."

87. Envision a similar scenario in which the patient consciously guesses the wrong symbols in order to be released from the program. This is not due to fear, but because they are a criminal who has been using information they learn from others for their own terrible deeds.

88. An unnamed character lies on the table, fear evident in their eyes as the shaman looms over them. "And this will

take away all the cancer?" the character asks apprehensively. The shaman nods, and waves their hands back and forth. The character cries out in pain as their stomach begins to open without anyone touching it.

89.   Envision a similar scenario in which an unnamed character has been taken against their will. They have no disease to speak of, and their body is only used as a training tool for an up and coming psychic healer. With their body laid open, they moan pitifully as the healer pulls out shards of glass, black balls of hair, and other strange substances from inside their guts.

90.   An unnamed character is walking casually down the street when the person next to them begins screaming. The unnamed character ducks behind a parked car just as the stranger bursts into flames.

91.   While browsing online, a new window pops up without the user clicking on anything. On the new page a series of words begins to scroll across. "THEY R COMING 4 U." The character thinks it's some kind of bizarre joke. That's when there's a knock at the door.

92.   A rookie policeman is called to a scene of a crime in which no one is sure if a crime has actually been committed. Upon arriving the rookie is told to observe the senior

officer as they make notes. "Strangest thing," the senior officer mutters while looking at the charred remains of a once vibrant human being. Stranger still, this is the fifth case and in all incidences, the owner was alone behind a locked door. Is this some kind of psychic murder, spontaneous human combustion, or something else entirely?

93. Thousands watch as an entirely nude individual gets off the helicopter and walks across the frozen tundra. It's a display to prove mind over matter. Craft a narrative from the perspective of this person or a spectator. Up next, the individual will go straight into an active volcano.

94. An unnamed character is busy at work when they get a horrible feeling in the pit of their stomach. From somewhere in the back of their mind they can hear their child's cries for help. Knowing that the child should have gotten home by now the parent frantically calls, but there's no answer. It turns out to be every parent's worst nightmare – their child has gone missing.

95. There is one theory which states that individuals with a great deal of anxiety are more prone to psychic ability, as their brain is naturally operating on a different wave of existence. Craft a narrative in which this is true. An individual has been extremely stressed at work, and then,

without warning, they begin to hear the thoughts of all of their co-workers.

96. While at a coffee shop one day, an unnamed character is approached by a very nervous looking individual. When the individual walks up the character is startled. This is the same person they have been dreaming about for years. The problem is, sometimes the dreams are nightmares.

97. A vigilante receives an IM from someone believing them to be a teenage girl. After receiving illicit photos and a few disturbing messages, the unnamed character logs off. Through their psychic connection they now have a target and soon they're on their way to the culprit.

98. While sleeping, an unnamed character is woken to the sound of someone breaking down their door. Before they have a chance to react, several officers with guns drawn burst through. "Is that the one?" one of them asks a strange grizzled man in a robe. The man closes his eyes and hums loudly, before finally nodding. The officers begin to shoot.

99. Since they were little, an unnamed character has noticed that the weather changes with their mood. First, it started off as small drizzles when they were sad, a little bit of lightening when they were angry, and dissolving clouds

when they were starting to feel happy again. However, as they get older not only do they find this strange phenomenon hard to control, but the weather is also becoming more intense.

100. An unnamed character wakes up from a cold sweat in the middle of the night. In their dream, a drowning woman calls out to them. Strangely, her hands are bound and it is when she is going down, down, down that the character wakes up. Chalking it up to a weird nightmare they are shocked the next morning when they turn on the news and see the woman's picture.

101. A well known police psychic is working a case when they receive the strangest vision they've ever had – themselves standing over the body of the victim with a bloody knife. The victim is unfamiliar, so it can't be connected to a case they are working on. Then, one day a new detective inquires about having the psychic help them out on an investigation. It just so happens the detective is the victim in their vision.

102. An unnamed named character gets an intense migraine while babysitting for the very first time. They take a few Advils and try to put on their best face. At the end of the day, when the child goes to hug them the character lets

out a small cry of pain as the child's life flashes before their eyes. Soon, it happens with other children too.

103. An unnamed character checks their watch and then nervously waits for the criminal to pass by. When the criminal does, the character pretends to be occupied by something else entirely, so the murderer grabs them and starts to brutally attack them. The character lets a small series of cries, but they are not surprised. They knew this would happen, and after a life time of having this strange ability, one they did not want, they are ready.

104. After being struck by lightning, an unnamed character begins to hear a strange buzzing sound whenever they are around certain people. Little do they know, the strange buzzing occurs only when someone is about to perish.

105. Envision the above scenario, however instead of this strange buzzing occurring only when someone is about to die, instead it occurs whenever someone has committed murder.

106. It has been three years since an unnamed character has had an usual psychic thought. The thoughts have ranged from being privy to a murder taking place to having an inner sense of when it is going to storm. Then one day, out of the blue, they have a sudden surge of every

premonition that they should have had over the past few years.

107.   Sitting alone in their room an unnamed character begins to gesture methodically to empty air. On the other side of the world a stranger drops dead.

108.   A psychic has been using their ability to win countless lotteries, horse races, and sporting bets to amass a small fortune. However, lately their visions have become increasingly bizarre to the point where it slowly drives them mad. Is this karma or something else?

109.   All their life, two twins have felt what the other has felt down to getting the exact same colds. Unfortunately, one tragic day one of the twins is in a horrible accident and slips into a coma and dies. The other twin swears that they can feel tiny pinpricks all over their body, followed by the feeling of flames.

110.   An unnamed character stares across the table at the psychic in front of them. "Are you sure this will work?" They ask hesitantly. The psychic nods and then takes the character's hands, closing their mind and trying to mentally remove the disturbing thoughts that have plagued the character.

111.   An unnamed character has the ability to smell death no matter how long ago it occurred. Generally, they can sense when it is old or more recent, which rarely ever happens. After a long day at work they come home to find the smell overpowering, but they can't seem to find a body.

Shadow People

In scientific terms, there has been a great deal of speculation surrounding the fourth dimensions and planes of existences humans do not perceive. Although the research is limited, in the paranormal facet there is the push for the idea that these dimensions are not only a reality, but they also may be compromised of whole worlds. Within those worlds strange creatures and beings may just emerge.

112.   The sound of drumbeats pour across the African plane. BOOM BOOM BAM, BOOM BOOM BAM. The sound intensifies as the painted bodies of men and women stare into the angry maw of the flickering fire. The smoke billowing out begins to elongate and shift, undulating into a new form. Before long the figure takes on a human shape and the drumbeats suddenly stop, waiting for the thing to speak.

113.   A young teen spends all night reading scary stories on the internet. Just as they are about to nod off, they see the screen begin to flicker and then turn off completely.

Assuming the computer is overheated, the teen is about to call it a night and go to bed. That's when the outline of a face appears on the screen.

114. An unnamed character visits a psychologist to get help after seeing the same dark figure, standing in the doorway of their bedroom, night after night for years. When they are finished telling the story the psychologist produces a drawing and asks if that is the figure they have seen. "Yes! That's it!" Turns out, this is a phenomena happening all over the world.

115. An unnamed character wakes up in the middle of the night to a strange voice in the room. Too tired to be terrified, they sit up to see a shadow in the corner of the room. The shadow beckons them forward, and when the character approaches, the shadow rushes towards them; intent on trading places and finding a space in this world.

116. "Hat Man" is a real occurrence that has been seen the world over. In fact, this legend is partially the basis for Wes Craven's "Freddy Krueger" character. True to the name, this shadowy being is simply a masculine figure that often wears a hat (typically in the style of a bowler hat). Imagine that an unnamed character sees Hat Man for the very first time, and has something the being wants.

117. While walking upstairs to go to their room, a teen character sees something out of the corner of their eye in the living room. When they turn their head – it's gone. Sufficiently creeped out, the teen rushes to bed, but when they turn off the light, the same shadow is now at the foot of the bed.

118. A young child loves to draw; often colorful pictures of puppies, kitties, their parents, and sometimes their friends. However, the child's drawings become significantly darker until one day all of the drawings are of the same pitch black shadow figure. When questioned by their parents, the child simply responds, "That's the monster that wants to eat you."

119. A group of scientists are working on dimensional planes, hoping to find, or at least recreate, a 4th dimension. However, there is an accident. Instead of creating a new plane of existence, the scientists inadvertently opens a door that allows beings to travel to ours.

120. While walking home from school one evening an unnamed character gets the feeling that something is following them. At first they are annoyed, thinking it might be a vagrant looking for a handout, but when they turn around – no one is there. Before long they realize that no one is following them, that is...no one other than

their own shadow, which has suddenly taken on a life of its own.

121. Just before their grandparent's death a young child receives a music box with the strict instructions never to open it at night. The young character, being a child, decides to do just that. As soon as the music begins to play a collection of shadows can be seen from the light emitting from the box, and soon they began to contort into horrifying figures.

122. One night, just as they are falling asleep, an unnamed character sees a frightening shadow looming over them. Instantly they wake up fully, but the shadow is gone. The next night the same thing happens, then the next and the next. Before long the character can no longer sleep and is starting to hallucinate even while being fully awake. As it turns out, that's exactly what the shadow wants.

123. During a train ride at night, an unnamed character decides to look out the window to take a break from the book they are reading. There, the character begins to see strange shadows in the trees, that only seem to grow larger and more menacing. The character tries to alert someone else, but no one else seems to see anything.

124. After a busy day at work an unnamed character comes home to relax and sit in front of the TV. It isn't long before they angrily begin to adjust the TV settings. It seems every single character, on every channel, has been replaced by a black silhouette. After being unable to fix the problem the character decides to log online, but once again – every human figure turns into a silhouette. Then the figures start to come alive.

125. Imagine a similar scenario, but instead, suppose it is everyone the character interacts with that looks like a strange black silhouette. Then pen what their mental demise might be like; or if they might have somehow tapped into an alternate dimension.

126. After being sideswiped by a passing truck, an unnamed character crashes into the forest. There, they see strange shadows reflected from the moonlight. Fearing they have a head injury they try to get back to safety, but the shadowy beings lure them further into the forest.

127. An unnamed character is walking down the hallway when they see a figure out of the corner of their eye. Quickly glancing over they see that no one is there, but that is exactly what the shadow wants them to think.

128.   Every full moon an unnamed character catches wind of a strange occurrence. Shadows that only they can see begin to frolic in the moonlight. When no one believes the character there is only one thing left to do – join them.

129.   Traditionally, shadow people are dark figures that are hardly ever seen. However, suppose humankind has finally caught wind of their existence and now activists want them to be protected no matter what the cost.

130.   Shadow people often take humanoid shapes and figures. Crush this trope. Envision a story in which these are not shadow people at all, but shadow *creatures* straight from the depths of your nightmares.

131.   While taking a short cut through a local cemetery an unnamed character sees the outline of a figure standing near an old oak tree. Frightened, the character hurries away, but from then on they continue to see this strange outline whenever they are not looking. Curiously, they research the cemetery only to discover they've found the location of an old hanging tree.

132.   An unnamed character is having breakfast with their parents on a casual weekend day. Suddenly, their parents start acting strange, attempting to hurt the hapless character. Without warning their forms begin to dissolve

right before the character's eyes until all that remains are grotesque shadows.

133.   An unnamed character gets good grades in school and has never been in any kind of trouble. However, one day they begin to act strangely; even a little unnatural. Very slowly do the others in their life realize that it isn't the character at all, but the shadow version of them.

134.   A young teenager begins to act strangely, claiming that shadow people are making them act irrationally and even a little bit insane. Eventually, the hapless character threatens to take their own life, with the audience never knowing if the character is truly seeing these strange beings or not.

135.   An unnamed character receives a call in the dead of night. When they answer it, they are greeted with a raspy voice that says simply, "This is the shadow man and you are going to die tonight." Thinking it's a prank the character hangs up and blocks the number. Little do they know, there's a silhouette in the window.

136.   A young unnamed character sees a shadow person when they are little, however due to their toddler mind they do not perceive the entity as bad or good. Every few years, however, they continue to see the figure, and their fear

continues to grow. The shadow person never makes a move, only watches. Then on the child's 18th birthday the figure finally says what it wants.

137. An unnamed character awakens from their nap by the sound of screaming. Instantly they rush to see what is wrong only to find the cries are coming from a silhouette in the shape of a woman.

138. A young unnamed character receives a strange lightbox for their birthday. They are warned never to use it on a full moon. Not only do they fail to listen, but when shadows are cast on the semi-darkened wall they suddenly become real.

139. Young parents have finally taken the plunge of letting their baby sleep in the next room. After finally dozing off with the monitor still on, they are awoken to a strange crackling sound. Rushing in to the baby's room they are shocked to see the infant being cradled by a large menacing shadow.

140. An unnamed character has eye problems that become increasingly worse. They go to the doctor and receive a pair of special glasses. Although their vision is now perfect they can also see strange beings that were not there before.

141. Most depictions of shadow people are *black* in color, but why do they have to be? Envision a scenario in which an unnamed character comes across a white shadow creature, or red, blue, etc.

142. While in a deep slumber an unnamed character is suddenly awakened by the sound of a door being creaked open. Standing in the doorway is a black shadow form, made more prominent with the light illuminated from the hall.

143. One of the more popular theories on shadow people is that they are actually visitors from a parallel dimension. Envision a scenario in which this is true and an unnamed character has been tasked with making contact; however these beings are anything but friendly.

144. A patient comes to the doctor's office complaining that a shadowy being continues to "sit on my chest and choke me." The doctor believes it to be a part of a mental disorder and prescribes some medication for the delusion. When the patient can no longer see these shadow people the beings decide that they must find someone else to torment, settling on the doctor.

145. Many individuals believe that the shadow people phenomenon is brought on by extreme fatigue and the

lack of sleep makes one see things that aren't there. Suppose this is happening to an unnamed character. Focus on their dissent into madness and the way they might see more and more strange shadowy figures.

146. A writer begins researching the phenomenon of shadow people. They begin to find hundreds upon hundreds of shadow people drawings amongst their patients. They cannot deny the similarity. It isn't shadow *people* the world has been dealing with, but a lone shadow person.

147. In a similar scenario, suppose the writer finds interesting tidbits of shadow people on the internet. They do not realize something is in the room watching them. As it turns out, the shadow people do not want to be found out, or researched.

148. Many individuals have heard the idea of a monster living under a child's bed. Suppose these are not monsters at all, but rather shadow people. This is why adults cannot see them – when they look under the bed the shadow people turn back into the darkness so that adults are none the wiser.

149. Envision a scenario in which shadow people are simply individuals who have passed on, but for some reason or other cannot find peace in death because of some

unfinished business. Now suppose an unnamed character has been tasked with helping them out.

150.   In Islamic mythology there are paranormal creatures known as jinn that greatly resemble shadow people, but are often made of smoke and fire. In this scenario, an unnamed character has met such an entity and must decide whether they are benevolent or downright evil.

151.   While waiting on death row an unnamed character suddenly begins to see shadow people. As the date approaches they see more and more strange beings until the moment right before death. That is when the beings are suddenly clear and have a message for them.

Ghosts

The concept of souls, spirits, ghouls, specters, phantoms, and any other name these otherworldly manifestations have come to be called, has existed throughout centuries. The belief that death simply cannot be the end to the human lifespan has been so engrained in many different cultures that the belief in these apparitions doesn't seem so out-of-the-ordinary, even if they can be a little bit frightening.

152.   It was a game. A stupid children's game that caused the teens to gather around the Ouija board and call out the name of Mad Jack McCarthy, a 18th century serial killer that murdered his victims with a meat hook. It was just a

game. That is until the gr gr k k grkkk sound of metal scraping against the old wood panelling can be heard from somewhere down the hall.

153. An unnamed character has a strange feeling that something is wrong. They check their children, but all are safe and sound. Then they check the unused nursery. There, the baby is choking in its crib. The biggest problem? Their youngest has died three years earlier.

154. An unnamed character has died from a traumatic event, say a murder or car crash. Craft a narrative in which they are not only slow to realize this fact, but they must now help someone else find their dead body.

155. Many Texans are aware of the bus legend in San Antonio. The tale goes that, some time ago, a school bus stalled on the railroad tracks and when a speeding train came by, every child on board perished. Even today, thrill seekers will stop on the track, put their car in neutral, and get pushed safely across. One might even see tiny handprints if they use some type of flour or dust on the back of their car. Use this scenario and craft a tale in which an unnamed character takes this dare and inadvertently brings these ghosts back home.

156. After the accidental death of their sibling an unnamed character begins to have terrible dreams, prominently featuring their deceased loved one blaming the character for their death. Each time the character wakes their sibling's picture is in a different place.

157. An unnamed character visits the grave of a recently departed loved one. With tears streaming down their face they run a hand over the hard, stone surface only to have someone place a sympathetic hand on their shoulder. When they look over they see the recently departed standing behind them.

158. In a similar scenario, perhaps the unnamed character is actually the recently deceased and it is they who wish to comfort a loved one.

159. An unnamed character is having an earnest chat with an elderly individual at the bus stop. After getting some wisdom that they desperately needed to hear, the elderly individual walks off the bus. It isn't until they are gone out of view that others on the bus began to ask who they were talking to. As the character looks back out the window they see the bus stop replaced by a cemetery.

160. During one particularly rainy day an unnamed character is walking by an old oak tree. Suddenly a grizzled man

approaches them, gun in hand, and wants, "all o' your money." Curiously, the man has the remnants of a rope around their neck. Just like that, they disappear before a further threat is made. Later the character discovers that this spot was the hanging tree made famous by the execution of One Eyed Billy, the famous outlaw, who died in the 1800s.

161. An unnamed character hears murmuring coming from inside the pantry. When they open it a ghost is hungrily eating all of their food. How is this possible?

162. An unnamed character is walking home in the rain when they are offered a ride from a very kind faced individual. Wanting to get out of the bad weather, the character tentatively accepts, only to find the temperature drop even further once inside the vehicle. After they are dropped off they see a news report featuring a story about a horrific car crash with no survivors. Then they see a photo bearing the face of the kind Samaritan that just gave them a ride home.

163. While staying at a bed and breakfast an unnamed character is given a room that is supposedly haunted. They don't believe the legend until they awake in the middle of the night to a ghostly visitor.

164. After losing a child an unnamed character has the hard job of going through all of their belongings. Before long they pull out an old worn bear and hear the sound of laughter. It turns out the deceased has come to visit them one last time.

165. An unnamed character hears the sound of a familiar barking outside their kitchen door. The only problem? Their dear departed pup has been gone for quite some time.

166. After responding to a singles ad an unnamed character goes on a date with a very attractive individual. In fact, they seem pretty much perfect; except for their eyes. Their cold dead eyes.

167. An unnamed character takes a wrong turn in an old hotel lobby and enters a hall they've never been in before. Before them a group of translucent people are walking from one end of the hall to the other, over and over again. At once, the ghosts stop and turn to look at the character. What do they want?

168. A rather nerdy unnamed character has decided to attend prom even though they have no date. They become drawn to a stranger that does not attend the school and the two

seem to hit it off. Very soon the unnamed character realizes that no one else can see this strange spectre.

169.   After receiving their first babysitting job, an unnamed character is in charge of a child that has trouble sleeping. When prompted, the child claims there is a human hand in the closet. When asked where the rest of the body is the child claims, "Right behind you."

170.   A mobile app is invented that will allow users to see ghosts in their house. Instantly sales start piling up. Who doesn't want to know if they are sharing their home with spirits? What manufacturers fail to realize is that these restless spirits do not want to be seen and once they are, there'll be hell to pay.

171.   An unnamed character finds themselves lost in the middle of a city at night. They know they need to ask for directions, but the first person they find isn't exactly alive.

172.   Imagine a similar scenario, but instead of an individual ghost, your character finds a whole section of the city composed of nothing but the recently departed.

173.   After years of trying, a scientist is finally able to capture ghosts. However, what they don't realize is that once a

ghost is captured they can then pass over to the mortal plane and attack the living.

174.   After a horrific car accident an unnamed character escapes their wreckage of a vehicle and tries to get some help. After finding no one, they circle back only to discover their own dead body being loaded on to a gurney.

175.   In a similar scenario, imagine that a character has unfortunately decided to end their own life. Not only have they succeeded but they are slow to realize that they are now a ghost and must prevent someone else from suffering the same horrible fate.

176.   An unnamed character is a horrible animal abuser that makes it a point to use helpless creatures as target practice. Once finished they simply dump the bodies in a spot out in the woods near their home. One day they hear the sound of scratching from somewhere outside. It gets louder and louder until the sound is suddenly all around them.

177.   After a brutal attack an unnamed character succumbs to their injuries and dies. Now in ghost form they must convince another person to help them get revenge on their murderer. For a variation, the character can choose to get revenge on their own.

178.   While reading about ghost stories an unnamed character
        falls asleep only to be woken up in the middle of the night
        by one of the haunting beings in the story they've just
        read.

179.   A small child is sitting in the kitchen when suddenly they
        start to yell at something in the corner. Their parent
        demands to know what is going on, but all the child can
        say is that the other kid is mad at them. There's no one
        there.

180.   An unnamed character has a very dark secret; they've
        murdered someone. Well, several someones. They believe
        that they will get away with it, but their ghostly victims
        have another idea.

181.   An unnamed character finds themselves walking along a
        lonely desolate road at night. A figure soon approaches
        them, asking them for directions to the "new world." It
        isn't until later that the character realizes that this was a
        deceased individual who needs to find solace in the
        afterlife.

182.   A police officer is constantly tormented by memories of
        the child they have killed. Even though they have been
        excused of all wrongdoing by the law, they are still filled

with the deepest regret because they know what really happened that night. Then the ghost of the child themselves shows up to forgive them.

183. An unnamed character falls asleep with their TV on, only to be awoken later by the sound of a figure emerging from it. They immediately recognize it as one of their favorite celebrities, or rather...undead celebrity.

184. While revamping a historically famous building, an architecture decides to walk the length of it to get a better idea of how the new floor plan will work. Suddenly, the ground below them collapses and they find themselves inside a dank cave. Surrounding them is the souls of all the workers who have died during the construction.

185. A rancher who has made a living off of slaughtering animals for food suddenly finds themselves being haunted by the ghosts of the cattle that have been slain.

186. In tune with the aforementioned idea of animal ghosts, craft a narrative in which an unnamed character is haunted by the ghost of creature; be it former pet, a wild animal, or something else entirely. The spirit wants something that the character simply cannot give them. Life.

187. An unnamed character and a group of friends decide to explore an abandoned themepark with the hopes of finding a few thrills. Big mistake. They are soon face-to-face with a horde of tortured souls, all who have died due to the same thing. It seems urban exploring can be quite deadly.

188. In a similarly constructed scenario, suppose the group instead finds an old nuclear test facility. There, they are haunted by the souls of all who have perished in the radioactive explosion.

189. Poveglia is a real island that is often simply known as "plague island." Built by the Venetian government, its purpose was meant to house those infected by the plague. Thousands perished there completely isolated from their loved ones. Suppose a group of researchers attempt to study this island only to meet these plague-infested ghosts.

190. A small collection of ghost hunters are busy researching a supposedly haunted place. What most people don't realize is that they have been running a scam, trying to get people to fork over cash for allegedly stopping the nonexistent ghosts – that is until they work a case in which the ghosts are very much real.

Possessions

Typically, when speaking of possessions there are two main types: demonic and spirit. Demonic possession is a popular horror trope, both in fiction and other forms of media. It occurs when an evil entity possess the body of an unwilling victim a la *The Exorcist*. Spirit possession is slightly different in that there doesn't necessarily have to be any kind of connotation of negativity. The spirit possessing the hapless victim may actually be benevolent in nature. However, what makes this concept so terrifying is largely the nonconsensual aspect of the possession itself.

191.   It started with an old cassette tape from the 1980s. An unnamed character was told by the music store worker that it was from an underground band that had sounds that were "out of this world." After listening, the character starts to feel a little funny, like they themselves don't quite belong to the reality they know. The more they listen to the music the more they begin to lose touch with all sense of themselves.

192.   An unnamed character is having trouble with their spouse. Desperate to save the marriage they go to an old shaman that gives them a spell to try. The spell works, the spouse is as attentive and loyal as ever, but perhaps it works just a little too well.

193.   An unnamed character has been feeling physically ill for
        quite some time now. They assume it's a minor cold, but
        their situation gets worse and worse. Then one morning
        they begin throwing up profusely. It's the last of their soul
        being expelled from their body. Something else will be
        replacing it entirely.

194.   An unnamed character notices that their best friend has
        been acting a little strangely all week. Their odd behavior
        continues to grow weirder with each passing day. Finally,
        the character can take it no longer and decides to sneak
        into their house, hoping to find a clue that would shed
        some light on this new change. While rummaging
        through the items they find a box and inside is a human
        scalp.

195.   The whole town had always gossiped about the unnamed
        character's great aunt. She practiced in the dark arts, they
        claimed. A witch, they cried. Now that she's gone an
        unnamed character must go through her old possessions.
        They find an old book and when they open it to the first
        page the character feels a little funny. "I will teach them,"
        The character cries, reaching for hidden items underneath
        the floorboards. A place only the aunt would know of.
        "Gossiping about me that way. I'll show them alright."

196.   The gravedigger wiped the sweat off his brow and sighed. For over thirty years he'd probably buried thousands of folks and now his old bones were getting tired. He threw another clump of dirt into the hole and took another break. That's when he heard rattling coming from inside the casket. He wasn't one to be afraid; the sound probably came from a trapped squirrel. He scrambled down with some effort and pulled back to the heavy oak top, hopeful to free the trapped animal. A strange breeze came out then, and when the gravedigger came back up he was spry as twenty young men.

197.   An unnamed character stared into the flames in front of them. "Are you sure this will work?" they asked the wrinkled crone next to him. She nodded eagerly, "Oh yes, all of your wishes will now come true. You'll be the most popular, the most attractive, and everyone will bow before you." The character took a deep breath and began to chant. What the crone failed to mention was that the character would only be a vessel for a greater power.

198.   A penniless writer decides to write under a pseudonym in order to drum up potential sales. Little do they know, the name they've chosen is a writer who took their own life, facing a similar fate. When the writer begins to achieve unparalleled success they can't quite shake the feeling that their success isn't all their doing. Worse, they cannot

shake the inexplicable feeling of sadness that comes on suddenly.

199.   A group of children are going trick or treating during one cold and dreary Halloween night. One child slips away from the group and visits a darkened house that most avoid. When the child returns they begin to act a little strangely – almost like the occupant of the house one might say. For example, the child may act like an elderly recluse or the town drunk. Play around with who might be the owner of the house.

200.   Tired of their horrible life an unnamed character decides to take it into their own hands, ending it once and for all. When they commit the act they are suddenly looking through the eyes of another. Is this a case of possession or something else entirely?

201.   At work a group of employees are celebrating a brand new merger when the boss, whom isn't very well liked, suddenly collapses from a heart attack. At that very moment a crash of lightening causes the lights to go out. When the lights return one employee suddenly has a lot to say about the poor way the boss's body is being treated.

202.   Most possessions have negative connotations surrounding them. For instance, the possessed individual might be led

to commit acts of murder or other atrocities. Envision a scenario in which the opposite occurs, and a good natured and helpful spirit possesses the body of an evil individual. Which side will win out?

203.   A scientist desperately wants to discover the key to immortality. They use the recently deceased to see if they can perhaps bring them back to life, but one day it all goes wrong – horribly wrong. The dead come back to life, in a way, only they are using the scientist's body to do it.

204.   A young unnamed character has a reputation for being something of a mischief maker. They have stolen bikes, destroyed mailboxes, and been involved in various shenanigans around town. Then one day the character decides to deface a local gravestone while loitering in the cemetery. Bad move. The restless spirit is determined to teach them a lesson, even if they have climb right inside of them to do it.

205.   Typically, possession involves only one entity slipping inside a human body. Envision a scenario where an unnamed character must deal with several entities in their horrific possession.

206.   Every twenty years a group of ghosts are allowed to possess one human on the night of Halloween. In this

scenario, consider what the ghosts might do on this night, who they might possess, and how they might interact with one another because of it.

207. While out drinking in abandon houses a group of teens decide it will be fun to draw a satanic symbol and worship the dark lord. While they think their goofing is just that, they soon realize that the devil is very real and he's interested in possessing of their souls.

208. To change up the aforementioned prompt, consider a scenario in which the teens must decide amongst each other whose soul Satan will possess. Clearly, this might bring out the worst in the teens as they argue, but what other ways might they decide who will be the victim?

209. An unnamed character stumbles across an old looking beeping box while boarding an otherwise vacant train. As soon their fingers touch the object they suddenly have an innate knowledge of locomotive technology and an odd urge to rob the transport.

210. In the 1800s, cattle rustling ran rampant. Although mostly harmless, it could still cost a rancher a great deal of money. This time, the cost might be greater. When a cattle rustler cuts a wire fence they not only find a herd of cattle, but ones with glowing eyes and snarling, spitting mouths.

211.   The new President of the United States is charming and personable, yet…something seems off. One night a staff member finds the President doubled over in pain inside the oval office. "Save me," they whisper. They convulse a few times and then stand up straight, as if nothing has happened. Note: the scenario can take place with the world leader of your choice.

212.   An unnamed character has always been extremely well dressed and slick in appearance. However, soon their friends begin to notice them become more and more dishevelled. Finally, the friends launch an investigation only to be told that by their friend that, "the person you are looking for no longer inhabits this body."

213.   In a similar scenario, suppose one by one all of the character's friends are soon possessed by other entities. For a stranger tale, perhaps they are possessed by the same entity.

214.   Edward Mordake was a real historical figure from the 1800s. Legend has it that he had a parasitic twin fused into the back of his skull that would allegedly whisper to him. Suppose that this is not only the case, but it is possible for him to have eventually become possessed by this strange entity.

215.   After a night out with some of their friends, parents come home to find the babysitter missing and their newborn levitating several feet in the air. What could have possibly happened?

216.   After losing a few cases, a lawyer is visited by a spirit that offers them a deal – give up control over their body and never lose a case, or lose every case for the rest of their career. After several wins, others around the lawyer notice something is definitely off about them.

217.   Suppose the lawyer has decided not to give in and now has to change career paths because of their unfortunate luck. Further still, suppose the spirit decides to try some other way to possess them.

218.   After their child begins to display strange behavior, such as speaking in weird voices and attacking others, the parents are convinced that their child might be possessed. A priest performs several exorcisms, but the child isn't getting any better. Suppose the real horror comes from the fact that the child isn't possessed at all, but is rather mentally ill. How does this situation play out?

219.   An unnamed character decides to use an Ouija board to talk to someone that has passed on. They get in touch with

their loved one and everything seems to be going well, that is, until they realize that this isn't their loved one at all. By then it's too late and the malevolent spirit jumps inside of them.

220.   A young character continues to complain to their parents that there is a "stranger in the closet." Several times, the parents check the closet, allow the child to sleep in their bed, and generally try to quell their fears. However, very soon they exasperatedly try to get the child to stop imagining things. The next morning the child acts normal...somewhat. The complaints stop, but it still isn't quite them.

221.   It starts off with a dripping faucet before the light switches on and off with no one in the room. Then the unnamed character begins to hear their name repeated over and over again. Finally, they wake up in the middle of the night to see a dark figure trying to wrestle their way inside the character's body.

222.   Envision a scenario in which a character wakes up to find the entire world possessed by one entity seeking revenge on them. What could have caused this search for vengeance and how does the entity go about utilizing their new captives?

223. After a horrific case of possession the afflicted finally succumbs to madness and dies. Even though the body is nothing but a corpse, the entity inside refuses to give it up.

224. While visiting a local hospital for minor cuts and bruises a patient suddenly begins to act erratic, clawing and biting at both the staff and fellow patients alike. They also begin to scream things like, "Leave this body alone!" and "This one is ours now!"

225. It is believed that many objects can be possessed and even have malevolent spirits attached to them. Suppose that this is the case with an otherwise seemingly innocent doll, given to a child one unfortunate birthday.

226. While out jogging, an unnamed character is approached by a large dog who opens its maw and plainly says, "You will do my bidding. You will kill for me." Is this hapless dog possessed or is it the runner who's actually crazy?

227. An unnamed character is given an exorcism in order to expel evil entities. However, before all are gone the priest declares sadly, "I cannot remove the last. It is too powerful."

228. An unnamed character is approached by a strange man dressed in black, wearing a white collar. They claim that

they are trying to help one who is possessed by 9 demons and in order to drive them out 9 of the chosen must be called to help. The stranger claims that 8 have been found and that the character is the 9th.

229. An unnamed character meets an individual who does not speak their language. Despite the communication gap, the two become good friends until they are told that their new friend speaks no language known to man.

Hellish Servants

Although "demons" and "hell" often bear biblical and Judeo-Christian implications, there are many religions and cultures that deal with a traditional concept of evil creatures or beings that are said to do the work of some sinister overlord. In Christianity, demons take orders from the Devil. In Hinduism, supernatural entities that are evil are typically human souls that, because of karma, are left to wander aimlessly before they can be reborn. This section will try to deal with as many of these evil creatures as possible. Although care is taken to use the correct terminology, default terms like "demon", "hell", "evil spirit", etc. may also be used, but these can be substituted to whatever helps the narrative.

230. One thousand. That's how many souls the demonic entity needs to drag to hell before it will be released from its service. Most of them were easy, but after centuries the demon is becoming restless, lacking caution. Before long

it finds its 1,000th victim, and this one isn't going to go down without a fight.

231. While sleeping peacefully a child is lulled away by a sweet melodic voice. The child looks to their bedroom door thinking they might find an angel beckoning them, but instead find a demon standing there.

232. While on a fieldtrip to a historically significant landmark, a teacher decides to take a group photo of her class. However, when the film is developed the teacher sees a group of demonic entities standing behind the children.

233. The unnamed character should have used the restroom at the previous exit. Now there doesn't seem to be any gas station for the next few miles. Finally, they have no choice but pull over and dash off road. They happen to enter into a cemetery. To be respectful they try to go away from the gathered headstones, not realizing that they've just gone on top of the most ancient and ruined one. As result, they summon an ancient demon, in charge of punishing those who desecrate the dead.

234. After their significant other leaves them, an unnamed character decides to visit a psychic to see what the future might hold. When looking in the crystal ball the face of a horrifying creature appears. With a serious glint in their

eye the fortune teller cries, "You will never find love again. *IT* won't let you."

235.   The lull of the carnival is far too much for the young character to ignore. Although they have been warned against going, they decide to check it out anyway. This isn't like any place they've ever seen and soon they are enraptured by odd creatures that scurry back and forth. Finally, out steps a being with long horns jutting out from a black as night top hat. "Welcome," their voice booms, "To the carnival of hell!"

236.   In olden times, the Jack o' Lantern might have been used to ward off evil spirits. Envision a scenario in which a character unwittingly creates a Jack O' Lantern that has the opposite effect; it lures demons like a beacon.

237.   An unnamed character finds a will o' the wisp trail leading deep into the woods. Hoping to find a collection of fairies, and perhaps a wish or two, they follow the sparkling lights. It isn't fairies they find but something much older and far more frightening.

238.   Envision a scenario in which a demon decides to leave behind its hellish ways and live amongst the humans. It dons an authentic costume, but is soon discovered by an overzealous reporter. The demon must make a decision,

kill the snoop or try to convince the reporter to let them be.

239.   While working in a used bookstore an unnamed character finds a large tome that is older than anything in the shop. Opening it up to a page at random they find information on how to summon a demon. Grinning to themselves, they put the tome under their own shirt and try to sneak out.

240.   For several days, an unnamed character has heard the sound of growling that they can't quite place. At first they believe it's the neighbor dog, but then the noise becomes more and more bizarre. Finally, they cry to the ether, "come out already." They immediately get their wish and the demonic figure isn't like anything they could have ever imagined.

241.   For many weeks now an unnamed character has felt a general sense of dread in their brand new home. Strange occurrences happen almost every night. Then one morning they wake up with long claw-like scratches up and down their back. The marks seem to spell out "Shiloma", but who or what is that?

242.   The dictator's hand hovers tentatively over the round button, debating if the harm done to the planet might be

worth dropping the bombs. Beside them the demon of war whispers, "Do it." The button is pushed.

243. A young unnamed character hears ruckus outside of their bedroom window. Curiously, they look outside to find a group of demons sitting on top of a nearby fence. When the creatures see the child they snarl and hop off, making their way over.

244. Anyone who has seen cartoons might have witnessed a toon's inner moral compass shown on screen, often depicted by an angel and demon. Suppose that this display really happens behind the scenes and one unnamed character is finally privy to it.

245. An unnamed character claims they are being hunted by an evil demon. No one else can see the creature – that is, until it is much too late.

246. While playing outside an unnamed character finds a small puppy trapped in a drain. They take it home and nurse it back to health. That's when unusual and sometimes deadly things begin to happen. Turns out, this is no puppy, but a very sneaky demon.

247. For many horror writers, including Mary Shelley and Edgar Allen Poe, the painting "The Nightmare" by Henry

Fuseli is especially inspiring. It depicts a sleeping woman surrounded by two grotesque demons. Build a story around this woman and how she came to be tormented.

248. An unnamed character is an exorcist who is called out to cleanse a tormented family from demons that are said to be living in their home. Craft a narrative that showcases their perspective, underlining how they might go about expelling these entities.

249. While many demons wander the land, there are many cultures that believe demons can haunt the water. In this scenario, a group of fishermen are plagued by a demon that lives in the very waters they are trying to use.

250. After so many centuries of tormenting humans a demon decides they do not want to do the job anymore. As a result, their fellow demons decide to torment them instead.

251. In olden Europe, public executions often happened outside of the city. The belief was that in doing so evil spirits would wander outside of the city gates, rather than inside. Craft a scenario in which this is true, only the evil spirits begin to draw out demons, who can very well get inside the city.

252. A group of scientists have captured a real life demon. They keep the creature in a glass cage and study its physiology in order to understand what they deem the "demonicus sapien." Then one day the entity breaks free and it is not happy.

253. There is a demon, Andras, who is said to have the body of a demon and the head of an owl. Not only can this entity command thirty legions of its fellow spirits, but folklore dictates that it can also give advice on how to kill. Suppose an unnamed character does seek advice from this creature, but the results are the opposite of what is expected.

254. Many cultures believe that demons have specific ranks, even leaders that command others. Craft a narrative that explains how a lowly demon goes from the bottom of the chain to Satan's right hand.

255. Suppose that demons are not created but born. In this scenario picture a young demon who must learn the ropes: from possession to leading humans into temptation.

256. In ancient Egyptian culture Amon is a demon who can see both the past and future. Not necessarily evil, it can guide humans on how to live their lives. An unnamed character

comes across this ancient deity while digging around in the tombs. Suddenly they see so much potential with this entity's advice, but it comes with a price.

257.   An unnamed character falls madly in love with someone they meet by chance. Their romance escalates very quickly until this person is all that they can think of. Slowly others around them begin to realize that they did not fall in love with a person, but rather a demon.

258.   While visiting the grave of a loved one an unnamed character comes across a part of the cemetery that seems to hide all light. They decide to inspect it and when they do, they discover a portal to hell, allowing demons to come and go as they please.

259.   There are a number of different cultures that believe that every type of demon has been recorded in an undiscovered ancient tome. Suppose an unnamed character comes across this manuscript and then suddenly gains the ability to see these entities.

260.   Craft a narrative which follows one angel who has fallen from heaven. Why did they turn their back on everything they have ever known and what kind of physical change might take place?

261. An unnamed character runs a local occult store that sells many different types of amulets and talisman that are supposed to ward off all manners of evil. Of course, this individual does not actually believe in evil spirits, but preys off the paranoid and gullible. Then one day something happens to make them a true believer.

262. While out filming about the destruction of local forests a documentary crew comes across a strange creature wailing in the dead of night. As soon as they approach the entity the demon stirs and attacks, killing them all. The only thing left is the footage of what happened.

263. An unnamed character studying the occult comes across an ancient text that states there are two twin demons on opposite ends of the world. Each demon has only a certain amount of human souls to tempt and take, keeping the world in balance. However, the more the character studies the more they realize that this balance is beginning to break, with one demon becoming exceptionally greedy.

264. Jinn are evil spirits that are said to hide in dark areas, from caves to graveyards and any place where light is vacant. During a power outage an entire town is plagued by one jinn who seizes this momentary lapse in light.

265. One of the most horrifying places on earth is the catacombs underneath the streets Paris. It is not uncommon for many poor souls to be lost down there. While vacationing an unnamed character does not heed the advice of friends and goes into the catacombs. While exploring they begin to be chased by an unknown entity and eventually cannot find their way back out.

266. There are many evil spirits that are said to live in the woods. After housing development proceeds and new houses are built, the new homeowners are soon tormented by these restless entities.

267. A c-list, third rate magician is constantly trying to up the ante on their tricks hoping to make it to the big time. This time they decide to use black magic in order to summon a demon. It is so extreme it is bound to draw a crowd. However, the results don't turn out quite as expected and instead of summoning some dark entity the magician instead sends themselves to hell.

268. An unnamed character pays a visit to a friend in order to see how they are doing. However, when they get there the door is open and since the two are good friends, the character goes inside. There they see their friend slipping into human skin, their demon form showing in full force.

Fears, Paranoia, & Psychological Undertones.

All horror stems from primal fears. No matter what the subgenre, theme, trope, or even the entertainment medium, it is all based on the most basic fears of humanity. For horror writers, one of the most effective ways to craft a terrifying tale is to consider the fear that exists behind the perceived dangers themselves. For instance, inclusion of aliens may drive from the fear of the unknown. Fear of clowns represent a childhood loss. Corrupted vampires are our fear of unbridled or unfulfilled sexuality. While zombies hit on the fear of disease and being a slave to a governmental, ecological, or social system. However, sometimes the most effective horror can mean stripping away these common themes to focus on the fear itself. When that happens that fear can often be elevated because it takes center stage; holding a mirror up to our own mortality.

Madness

In short, insanity, craziness, or simply madness is the idea of an individual displaying some type of behavioral problem that is outside the scope of what is normally socially acceptable. Although there are real mental disorders that should not be taken light of, when popular horror fiction includes some form of abnormal behaviors, whether in the characters or as a central theme, this is often outside of what even these mental illnesses may create.

269. An unnamed character finds themselves awaking inside of a locked padded room wearing nothing but a strait jacket, a thin shirt and an even thinner pair of pants. Their head feels clogged and their memory is even more congested. As they shake themselves and stand to their feet they try to remember the last thing that happened to them. That is, before the sound of screaming rings out from somewhere down the hall.

270. At an upscale party an unnamed character feels a little feverish. They begin to sweat profusely and without warning they suddenly fall to the ground, grunting and moaning. As others, all dressed in their best, begin to crowd around the character one can't help but wonder – has something been put in their drink to make them act in such a way or is this the start of their own madness?

271. While on trial a defendant attempts to cry, giggle, and bark uncontrollably in an attempt to boost their insanity defence. Although they are clearly lying about their plight,

suppose they eventually do become mad from their efforts, but by then it's too late.

272.   An unnamed character is a real estate agent whose job requires inspecting houses after they have been foreclosed in order to determine resell value. While inspecting one house the agent is unfortunate to discover a corpse that was emaciated to death. There is a journal next to them detailing how and why they starved themselves in their own madness.

273.   A well respected King or Queen is slowly becoming mad. During their first two decades of rule they were known for their patience and mercy, but now they are known only for their harsh cruelty. The populace is torn between their love for who this leader was versus their hatred for what they have become.

274.   In a similar scenario, envision the above as a modern take. Suppose the President, or other world leader has become mad, but they have made an effort of hiding it from all others. What might happen if they declare war or cause allies to falter in their trust?

275.   An unnamed character wakes up to find themselves standing in a pool of blood in the kitchen. Nearby is someone very dear to them. They drop the knife they have

been holding and drop to their knees in anguish. However, is this a case of sleepwalking, madness, or something else entirely?

276. In order to cover their costs one mental facility has begun to film patients in a type of reality show. In this scenario, focus on the psychological horror that might come from not treating human beings with respect as well as the sociological undertones this would mean for those watching.

277. After years of fame and excess a world renowned painter becomes more and more of a recluse. Some even say they have gone mad. It isn't until they die that their last paintings show just how far gone their mind really was.

278. An unnamed character has made several attempts to be committed to a mental institution for various urges, such as the need to kill. However, each time they go the facility turns them down in order to lower costs. After all, involuntary commitment should take place over a voluntary plea. Then one day the character snaps altogether and takes their first life.

279. While in class, a usual quiet and well-respected student suddenly goes mad, screaming and throwing themselves around. Others begin to panic from the strange display,

before joining. What is the professor to do when the whole class has gone mad.

280. Anyone that has suffered from a panic attack can attest that they are exceptionally brutal. One can feel like they can't breathe, their hands are sweaty, chest is tight, and ultimately they feel like they are dying. An unnamed character has their first panic attack in the middle of a crowded location, but no one around them seems to want to render aid.

281. An unnamed character has been faithfully helping a loved one who often has fits of rage and madness. Although it can be considered borderline, if not outright, abusive they continue to try to muster through the pain. Then one day it is they who finally snap.

282. An unnamed teen character has recently learned that their entire family has been slaughtered while they were away being rebellious. The resulting guilt is driving them insane.

283. Envision a scenario in which an insane individual believes that they are normal and everyone else is crazy. They are so invested in this misguided belief that they are going to try to 'fix' everyone else, by any means necessary.

284. MK-ULTRA was an USA experiment that used civilians as lab rats; giving them LSD in various dosages to understand their effects. Craft a scenario that follows one hapless individual as they and others around them are suddenly feeling the effects of the drug, but have no idea it has been given to them.

285. After a major catastrophe, a mental facility has been almost destroyed save for a small group of survivors. An unnamed character is one such, but has no recollection of life before the event. Furthermore, they have no way of knowing if they were a patient or a staff member.

286. In a similar scenario, consider what might happen if only the patients with the most extreme cases of madness are left. Survival is a must, but how might they cope given their new circumstances?

287. An unnamed character is a staff member at one of the most notorious mental institutions. Unfortunately, it's notorious for all of the wrong reasons. The horror lies in the abuses that are seen and your character must find some way to stop it.

288. Suppose that your character does not work at the above facility, but is instead a patient there. They are going to

undertake a long journey to escape, but the task will not be easy.

289.   An unnamed character has been committed to an insane asylum for claiming they have some kind of super power. Their belief is so strong that one day it suddenly manifests.

290.   An unnamed character is in charge of tossing out the dead after experimentation gone wrong. The owner of the facility believes that the mad are the perfect subjects for such experiments. One night while the character is making their rounds the dead suddenly come to life, and they are not happy with how they have been treated.

291.   After a car accident an unnamed character slowly begins to have a personality change. Once they were known for their extreme kindness, but they are now known for their brutality. Including their urge to kill.

292.   While out exploring the more decayed parts of the city, an unnamed character comes across an old medical facility that has fallen into ruin and disrepair. Thinking it abandoned they get their camera ready and venture inside. Not only is it still in use, but the patients there are being used for organ harvesting.

293. More than a century ago, mental illness was misunderstood and regarded as some kind of work of the devil. Craft a scenario in which an unnamed character of this era is going to try to prove that these individuals not only deserve care, but it's also very possible they can be 'cured.'

294. An unnamed character begins to see a strange and haunting figure in the dead of night. They try to take some of their medicine, but this does not work. They reach out to their therapist, but they do not answer. The figure seems to be closing in.

295. After suffering a severe head injury an unnamed character begins to have wild mood swings. They might be extremely angry one minute and then deeply sorrowful the next. Although this in itself is bad enough very soon the character can no longer recognize themselves at all.

296. In order to live as 'normally' as possibly, an unnamed character must take several different types of pills a day or they might suffer a hallucination episode. They commit to the task and life improves for them. That is until the apocalypse hits and they have no way to acquire their medication.

297.   An unnamed character stumbles across someone who is attempting to jump off the side of a building. Unsure of what to do the character decides to climb up with them and possibly talk some sense into the individual. However, the more the would-be jumper talks to more sense they are beginning to make to the character.

298.   An unnamed character has been trying to help a friend overcome their mental issues with much difficulty. After years of trying to offer them some type of aid the friend finally decides to seek help. Too late does the unnamed character realize that they are actually an imaginary friend. If their companion gets help it would mean that the character would no longer exist.

299.   An unnamed character is forced into an institution to get help with the strange voices they hear. The first night is especially troubling because they soon meet another patient who claims to hear the exact same thing.

Medical Grief

It's the stuff of urban legends – a vacationer wakes up in a hotel room with a missing organ or two, a medical tourist tries to receive care from another country only to find it backfire horrifically, or perhaps, a strange pandemic takes hold, killing off the population one-by-one. The idea of medical grief, stems from a lot of different fears. The onset of a plague stems from our fear of real diseases that could potentially take hold. It also touches on our fears surrounding stolen body parts or improper care stemming from the fear of outsiders, piggybacking on xenophobia. While, fear of hospitals or doctors in general stems from our fear of losing control, aging, or dying. All of these elements work together to make the mere concept of something going wrong medically to be downright terrifying.

300. "Count down from 10 for me." At 10 the unnamed character is feeling a little apprehensive. By 5 they are drifting off to dreamland and by 2 they are already asleep. When they awake they open their mouth to utter the last number. It is then that they realize in horror that their tongue has gone missing.

301. An elderly individual has an intense and overwhelming fear of dying. So much so that they are using their retirement funds to find a way to live longer. They respond to an ad about a fountain of youth available deep in the mountains of Asia. Once there however they find that the elderly are not given eternal life, but rather they are being harvested.

302. An unnamed character has recently received their medical degree, but work is hard to come by. They decide to take up the first offer given to them, but it comes with a price – they must transplant organs "donated" by hapless victims.

303.   A pill is invented that will stop the aging process completely. However, it is only available in a remote part of the world, and although many believe the high price is strictly monetary, it's something else entirely.

304.   The high price of medicines have forced many to seek treatment elsewhere. Rather than cause this to bring prices down, it only escalates them further. As a result, many shady practitioners crop up and an unnamed character happens to pick the most diabolical of them all.

305.   Suppose an unnamed character has opted for plastic surgery and at first everything goes swimmingly. They are back home, they look great, but their good feeling doesn't last long. Before long their skin begins to bubble and within the week massive growths appear all over their body.

306.   A young child has had trouble dealing with a degenerating disease. So much so that they begin to invent an imaginary friend to help cope with the illness. This actually seems to work out well, that is until strange things begin to happen that would be impossible for the child to be responsible for.

307. An unnamed character works in the hospice section of the hospital wing. Since they have only recently been hired, they try to stay out of the way and learn about the culture from others. However, one night they stumble across one of the other orderlies taking advantage of the most vulnerable. Perhaps worse still, the orderly knows the character has spotted them and is very clear about what would happen if they tell anyone. This scenario can be changed and the culprit can take place in the cancer ward, the children's hall, and so forth.

308. In an attempt to cure a certain disease a researcher actually ends up doing the unthinkable – he allows the diseases to take a larger physical form and exist out of the body. As a collective unit these visible disease still have one thing on their mind – destroy humanity.

309. It begins with a lone sneeze in the middle of a crowded bus terminal. Three days later half of the world's population has been wiped out, and by the end of the week there is only a few survivors. They too are dying, all except one character who seems to be immune to this odd disease.

310. In a similar scenario, suppose that the majority of the world's population is gone and the rest are in the midst of dying. However, a cure is found but it is in very limited

supply. How might it be decided who gets to live and who does not?

311.	A disease moves through a small, remote island village. The surviving islanders are desperate to sail away, but soon find their boats have been destroyed by those that do not want the disease to spread to the mainland.

312.	An unnamed character finds themselves on an operating table, ready to undergo what they assume is life-saving surgery. Just before they are about to nod off, they hear one of the doctors asking if the other patients are ready to receive their new donor organs.

313.	In a different scenario, suppose an unnamed character is actually undergoing surgery that will help them. Everything is going great until they realize that they can hear the mundane chatter from the surgeons. It isn't until the first cut, which causes them to mentally scream out in agony, that they realize they have not been put under.

314.	An unnamed character visits a remote island as part of an anthropological study. Although they are there to study some benign part of the culture, they soon take note of a strange longhouse, several miles away from the camp in which several sick tribe members dwell. As it turns out, those who do wrong by the community are made to live there. Becoming infected by the others is simply part of the punishment.

315. An unnamed character wakes up one day to discover that they have a special gift. Their hugs can cure any ailment imaginable. They immediately begin to help others not realizing that their gift is finite, and it will eventually catch up to them.

316. An unnamed character is taken aback when a classmate begins to spit and foam at the mouth before breaking out into spasms. Others begin to follow suit before almost everyone in the classroom is collapsed on the ground.

317. Envision a scenario in which an unnamed character has reached the end of their life cycle because of an unfortunate disease. Craft a narrative of what might happen as they slip away and then after they pass completely. You can choose to focus only on their plight, or segue to the others they leave behind.

318. In order to help with the growing needs of organ transplants a new law has passed which allows assisted suicide. The catch is that the body they leave behind goes towards someone that needs it. Once a waver is signed the procedure commences. However, what happens when someone changes their mind?

319. There have been many cruel and inhumane experiments that humankind has undergone in order to make way for medical advances. Envision a scenario in which an unnamed character is an unwitting pioneer in one such instance.

320. A world renowned surgeon comes down with a life threatening disease that requires only the most delicate hands. Although there are many others that can do the procedure, the surgeon will not allow anyone else but themselves to perform the feat.

321. While away on vacation an unnamed character comes back to find that almost everyone in their hometown has perished because of an aggressive pneumonia that took hold while they were gone. How might they cope with the knowledge they survived by sheer luck?

322. All forms of diseases have been completely eradicated and most accidents, no matter how extreme, can be cured through medical technology. The population is four times what it is now and resources are dwindling down. An unnamed character is one of the collection of scientists that is going to create a bioweapon that can trim humanity to a more reasonable number. What could possibly go wrong?

323. In a similar scenario, suppose this bioweapon is the result of a terrorist attack and your character is but a cog in a machine much larger than them. How will they react when their family begins to perish and there's nothing they can do about it. Further still, how do they map out the rest of their own days.

324. An unnamed character is suddenly given a gift in which they can take someone's ailment and give it to someone else. They can easily use this gift for profit; perhaps taking an illness from someone and putting it on their enemy for a price, or they can use their new power for something else entirely.

325. An unnamed character is at one of the most elite hospitals on the planet when an individual comes in complaining of abdominal pain. Their symptoms soon escalate and before long, they are on the brink of death. Curiously, doctors have never seen anything quite like this before.

326. A small pup is taken to the vet with symptoms that have not been seen before. Soon, other animals are being brought in with similar ailments. Then, the first human case emerges.

327. An unnamed character is a young doctor who has a patient that comes in with something that looks suspiciously like the plague. Although it is in a new form entirely. Despite their efforts, much of the medical staff especially the higher ups, are not too keen on eliciting panic and try to keep the whole thing under wraps. That might be a big mistake.

328. News reports have been blasting all day about the global pandemic underway. Symptoms are described, response plans are mapped out, and the probable line of infection is drawn out. It is then that an unnamed character realizes that they are patient zero.

329. Perhaps one of the most horrifying themes that can be shown through the lenses of horror is what medical themes do to the people that are left behind. In this scenario envision an unnamed character that checks in on their parents, a monthly routine, only to discover they have been ill and have passed. Their death was clearly some time ago. In what ways would their guilt be amped up?

330. A great deal of concern is often placed on disease prevention. In this scenario suppose parents are checking the genetics of their child as a preventive measure.

Startling, the child displays a genetic anomaly that makes them immune to all diseases on earth.

331.   A new strain of disease has descended upon humankind. However, it isn't a prion, virus, bacteria, or any known entity. Just what is it?

332.   As an exercise on expanding your skills as a creative, look up a medical ailment you are unfamiliar with. The more obscure the better. Once you have something in mind craft a narrative from the perspective of the afflicted. Particularly consider what their day-to-day life might be like and how they might be treated by others.

333.   An unnamed character receives a care package from a neighbor they have previously been at odds with. Little do they know, all of the goodies have been laced with a sinister pathogen.

Isolation

Isolation deals with one of the most pressing phobias that humankind has – the fear of being alone. As empathetic creatures, it is our nature to want to communicate and build upon relationships with members of our own species; be it through families, friendships, or intimate relationships. When all that is taken away, it can be downright maddening.

334. Researching the melting icecaps, a group of environmental scientists are hit by a surprise snowstorm, one of the worst the crew has ever seen. During the aftermath, an unnamed character is unfortunate to find the other members of their crew deceased. Worse still, all communications systems are down and there is no telling when the next food package will arrive with more storms oncoming.

335. While exploring one of the remotest parts of the Amazon an explorer discovers a deep cave. They find the cavern by happenstance; falling straight down into it. Climbing back out would require scaling several yards up.

336. Suppose the unnamed character who has fallen into this ominous cave has broken a limb on the way down. It would only seem likely. With no one else around how might they make their way out despite their now useless appendage?

337. An unnamed character has been lost for days, searching endlessly for the trail back to safety. The more they move the deeper into the wilderness they find themselves. Craft a scenario in which this is purposeful and the forest is punishing them for some wrong done.

338. Stuck on a raft in the middle of an ocean, an unnamed character is on the brink of starvation. In fact, it is very likely that they will starve to death. In order to keep this from happening, they have a choice of eating the raw fish they can manage to bring on board or catching birds that chance by. Either way, they will have to tear into the flesh of a living creature.

339. Suppose a similar scenario is true, though the setting can be any isolated place. However, this time there is simply no food source at all. That is, nothing that exists outside their own body. When the character accidentally scrapes their skin they feel a familiar rumbling sensation in their stomach when the blood flows freely.

340. An unnamed character finds themselves being awoken by a loud pop and the smell of something burning. It is then that they feel the heat coming from a nearby fire. It isn't long until they are surrounded by the flames. With no one else in the house and being miles from the nearest neighbor, they have no idea if help will come in time.

341. While taking a hike in the late afternoon an unnamed character stumbles across an array of wild blueberries. Forgetting to pack a lunch and thinking they know everything there is to know about managing it alone in the wilderness they quickly gobble some up. It isn't long until

the first round of cramps hit them. Soon they are wondering further off trail, hallucinating and raving mad.

342. Up until now a prison inmate has been the pinnacle of good behavior. All that changes when they find themselves in the giving end of a large scale fight. As punishment they are thrown in isolation for the very first time.

343. A earthquake hits and an unnamed character is trapped under hundreds of feet of rubble. They can hear rescue workers, but they have no way to call for help.

344. An unnamed character wakes up in a completely dark room that is hot and stifling. Reaching forward they realize with horror that they are in a very confined space, enclosed on all sides. The air seems limiting and before long it is hard for them to breathe. It is in that moment they realize they've been buried alive.

345. A small child notices their parent or guardian has become quite ill. It started off as a small cough but within the week it has grown to a massive case of pneumonia. Horribly, the only adult in the house passes and the child is left to their own devices.

346. An unnamed character has been all alone since birth, being abandoned by their parents in a remote locale – be it the jungle, the slums of a city, and so forth. Craft a scenario in which this character stumbles across civilization for the first time and it's far worse than they could have imagined.

347. An unnamed character is enjoying a warm summer night on their back porch, hundreds of miles from another soul. In the distance, strange lights begin to blink from the woods. It seems to be in Morse code.

348. While walking home an unnamed character is attacked by a masked assailant. They assume they might be robbed, or worse. However, the perpetrator's M.O. is stranger than anything they could have ever imagined. Before the character knows it they find themselves in a plywood box with wet cement being poured over them.

349. An unnamed character has chosen to be alone, tiring of all of the drama in day-to-day life. They've taken a boat out to the middle of the ocean expecting to come back in a few months. However, once there they realize that isolation is not all it's cracked up to be, but there's a problem – they've gotten lost.

350. In an ancient tribe, a sacrifice must be made in order to appease the gods. An unnamed character has been selected and now they must ascend into the tallest mountain. Dying from exposure may be imminent, but it's what they deal with on the way to the top that would make for an interesting piece.

351. An unnamed character has been in a coma for over twenty years. However, that's just what everyone assumes. The reality is that the individual is fully conscious, but is unable to speak.

352. After a tiring jog an unnamed character decides to sit on a nearby bench in order to take a breather. However, when they get up they find that they cannot move at all! It seems they are stuck with no other soul in sight.

353. In a similar scenario, there have been documented cases of humans who have been fused to seats (chairs, sofas, toilets, etc.) because they have refused to move for some reason or another. Craft a tale in which an unnamed character has not gotten out of bed for several months, and now it seems like they may never again.

354. An unnamed character gets into a multicar accident while inside a usually busy tunnel. When the sounds of scraping

metal and screams stop they find that they might be the only survive. A trapped one at that.

355. Craft a scenario in which an individual, whether by torture or by disease, has lost all of their senses. What kind of horror might be wrought if they were truly alone, unable to connect with anyone else.

356. On a nature hike in a new place an unnamed character finds remnants of an abandoned carnival. Curiously, a large sign says "Beware all who enter." They decide not to heed it, and the more they walk they deeper into the fairgrounds they go. It's almost as if there is simply no escaping.

357. During what should have been a night of adult fun, an individual suffers a fatal heart attack leaving someone else still gagged and tied to the bed, with no way to call for help.

358. An illusionist has done this trick a million times over – encase themselves in a glass box for an entire month without food or water. However, this is all a rouse and they have a trap door which allows the passage of food and transportation of waste without anyone being the wiser. During this run however, the door has been glued

shut and there's no way to let anyone know without blowing their cover.

359.   While on a job interview, in a building they have never been in before, an unnamed character gets stuck on the elevator. At first it's only slightly annoying, but minutes turns to hours and then they begin to freak out. Soon...it's days.

360.   A pair of prisoners escape and are on their way to freedom. However, the prison is surrounded by a large desert and they are still handcuffed together. Before they can get the cuffs off one of the prisoners is suddenly bit by a venomous snake and death is imminent.

361.   These scenarios deal with those forced into isolation by no desire of their own. Envision a scenario that deals with the reverse end of the spectrum. An individual has lived in isolation for thirty years, but is now being forced into the modern world. Do they have a good reason for being shut away? Further, what might happen when they are put amongst the rest of the populace?

Social Themes

Closely related to the idea of madness or isolation, the concept of social themes seeks to break into the mold of what is deemed socially acceptable behavior. More often than not, it also touches on that inherent need to communicate and build upon relationships. What happens when social standards are broken completely?

362. It started with turning down offers to go out; a trip to the newest blockbuster release, out to a new fancy restaurant, and so on. Then it was refusal to do even the most mundane activities; the grocery store, getting gas, etc. By the end of the week, this unnamed character cannot bring themselves to leave the house, terrified of going beyond the front door, but not quite sure knowing why.

363. An unnamed character has always been a very talkative and personable individual. All of that seems to change after an intense storm. When the weather clears out the character no longer speaks. Are the two related or is their sudden muteness something else entirely?

364. During an exceptionally intense meeting an unnamed character jokingly says that it makes them want to "blow their brains out." Strangely a co-worker pulls out a gun, obviously smuggled into the building, and offers to help.

365. An unnamed character finds themselves one of the participants in a strange social experiment. One of the lead scientists says that they have all been subjected to a substance that will make them irrationally angry and violent. Almost all of the participants begin killing each

other and it is only later that the character discovers that there is no substance, they've been given a placebo.

366.   After a particularly mean-spirited comment they've made on the internet, an unnamed character begins to receive photos from an unknown number. First of their house, then of their family, and then gruesome photos of themselves, dead.

367.   In a similar scenario, suppose an unnamed character is a freelancer who has a particularly uncontrollable client. First, they are only mean and demanding, even going as far as threatening legal action (without basis of course), but then escalation occurs and the client begins to harass the character at work and even at home.

368.   A young unnamed character spends the night at a friend's home only to discover that the family has very strange and unusual customs. Not wanting to offend their friend, the character participates with a forced smile, even if in doing so they are engaging in rituals that might be deemed inappropriate anywhere else.

369.   While watching an old 1950s American sitcom, an unnamed character falls asleep and suddenly awakens in that world. Everyone in the era has set manners and identifies with the social norms and customs of the day.

The character tries to fit in, but it isn't long before their "rude" behavior becomes notable. Then, when someone assists the character and they do not say "Thank you" the townsfolk have had enough and death seems certain.

370. An unnamed character has always wanted children of their own, but sadly it's never quite happened for them. Then one day they go off the deep end and soon others can see the character tending to a very realistic looking doll. A little *too* realistic.

371. A misogynistic rape-enabler constantly fights for their rights as the most dominate in society on internet forums. They seem to be invincible behind a keyboard, but that changes when they wake up drugged and dressed up in a doll costume, chained to an alley wall. Before they truly understand what is happening, they hear footsteps nearby.

372. A prosecutor gets a horrific case about a child who has been murdered because their parents can't seem to stop their "bad manners." Rather than using their prowess on the court the prosecutor decides to take the law into their own hands.

373. Deep within a small, Texas town circa the 1920s a racist shop owner suddenly finds themselves the target of

lynching. In this tale of karmic revenge focus especially on what turn events have lead them to this moment.

374. An unnamed character has always been the type of person to want to please others. In fact, others might notice that they have a habit of apologizing quite often, whether or not they have truly done anything wrong. One day they tire of being such a subservient person and decide it is they that will be in charge, no matter what.

375. Every midnight an unnamed character goes to the rooftop and starts singing at the top of their lungs. Despite numerous complaints and visits from local law enforcement the singing continues to the point where everyone simply ignores the odd behavior. Then one night, the singing stops completely. Despite being relieved the real question is – why?

376. Through a botched time-travel experiment, a scientist finds themselves in a strange future where, though society is technologically advanced, the social atmosphere is completely barbaric. They must survive in an era where murder is common and regarded as an insignificant but necessary solution to everyday problems.

377. An old socialite constantly complains to their caretakers about the glory days and how everyone these days have no

respect for anyone or anything. One by one caretakers come and go, then one day there is a helper who decides they will teach this elderly crone a thing or two about respect.

378. In order to test one's mental state, handwriting of murderers and serial killers are often studied. More often than not many use the "Devil's Fork", a series of smaller dashes against a long line akin to a fork, when writing. Suppose that an average, everyday person suddenly starts to display this strange marking when writing.

379. While on vacation, a family meets some locals that are quite taken aback by some of the behaviors that the family displays. Unperturbed the family continues to act the same way they've always done; that is until the local community is going to force their hand into "normalcy."

380. An unnamed character cannot stop cleaning. They mop the floors, scrub the walls, wash the windows, and yet they still feel like the place is still too dirty. Since they cannot seem to stop, would it be possible that they might just clean themselves to death?

381. An unnamed character is a convict in a dystopian society that is given a surprisingly common sentence of public suicide in front of an audience of family, friends, and the

entirety of the local population. The alternative to this barbaric act is to have those same loved ones killed.

382.   An unnamed character has trouble fitting in no matter what social circle they try. It has been this way since they were a child. Now that they are an adult they have decided to make their own friend group, whether or not those find actually want to be in it.

383.   Down on their luck and looking for a job, an unnamed character applies for a housekeeping position for a wealthy socialite, but is forced to be a "human pet" to an abusive and manipulative "owner".

384.   An unnamed character lives in a society where women kill men after successful mating, akin to many types of bugs. A man who had been unsuccessful in impregnating anyone for years is horrified to find one woman holding a positive pregnancy test. Although this particular prompt is tied to gender, feel free to play around with this scenario in any way that you choose.

385.   A teacher is in hot water when they are found punishing the children who have been a nuisance in their classroom. Rather than simply reprimand them with the loss of their job or a warning, the principal has a different idea entirely.

386.   In a town where the amount of children has just been legally restricted to two, a young unnamed character has just overheard a local official tell their parent that they will have to be killed because they are the least likely to survive as an adult. The small character doesn't think their parent would actually heed the sheriff's advice, until they see their parent sitting at the kitchen table, sharpening a knife.

Uncontrollable Areas

There are some horror concepts that stem from the fear of isolation or being separated in a social setting, but are unique in their own way. These are special circumstances that have gone completely awry. For instance, being hit by car because of the other driver, slipping and falling into a ravine full of crocodiles, and so on. One of the most common themes that deal with this type of horror is claustrophobia, the fear of tight spaces, or acrophobia, the fear of heights. One's inability to control what happens in these areas is often what makes them so deadly afraid of it.

387.   A group of unnamed characters are exploring a vacant fairground when one of them suggests sitting on the Ferris wheel and taking a few pictures. Once seated, another friend decides to crank an old lever that causes the great monolith to turn, albeit slowly. The characters seated think nothing of it, that is until they get to the very

top and their friend, who should be turning the lever by now, suddenly drops dead from a heart attack.

388. There is a section of Mt. Everest known as the "Dead Zone" in which the corpses of ill-fated travellers are strung about. The area is far too dangerous for them to be retrieved and thus, in many cases they act as a marker so that one knows what section of the mountain they are in. Amongst these, the most famous is "green boots", a corpse known for the neon boots he wore in life. Craft a scenario in which a character has stumbled across this infamous mountaineer and has run out of oxygen. The body is a reminder of what will happen if they don't find help fast.

389. After accidentally starting a forest fire, a group of campers must escape their tent before they're all burned alive, but an unseen force won't let them leave.

390. In olden times, a cruel ruler is finally dethroned and must pay the ultimate sacrifice – being walled up alive in their own throne room. Envision a scene in which an unnamed character is such a ruler and will spend the rest of their days in the darkness of their own making.

391. An artificially made hybrid animal is accidentally set loose in a private lab facility, a scientist must survive being

hunted by this superior beast after all others have been killed by it. No matter where they run, the beast seems always behind them. It won't be long before both human and beast run out of food.

392.   After a horrific car crash leaves every passenger, but themselves dead, an unnamed character struggles to survive. Supplies are dwindling and they have an injury that requires immediate assistance. What's worse is that they have no idea where they are.

393.   Suppose in a similar scenario, an unnamed character is the driver who has caused the horrific incident. Since the other car has careened off road, deep in the foliage where it will not be discovered, the only evidence might be the group of bodies strewn across the road. The character decides to hide the evidence, but when they drag the last body off road they suddenly feel something grab at their leg.

394.   A group of survivors have managed to pull themselves out of a wreckage of a plane crash. Since they are in the middle of nowhere, there is no doubt that help will take time to arrive. Within hours the group already begins to turn on each other in murderous fits of rage.

395. While working as gravediggers, two unnamed characters get into a petty argument and start to fight right over the grave of the deceased. During one hard shove the two manage to unwittingly fall into a coffin that just so happens to be extra large due to a mix-up, in which a couples coffin was used. If landing on top of an already decomposing individual isn't bad enough, the two grave keeps inadvertently cause the coffin lid to shut behind them. It's too bad this is in the 1800s when coffins are auto-locking.

396. A group of unnamed characters decide on a whim to explore some abandoned trains near their home. At first the group doesn't find anything of interest, but soon they find themselves trapped in one of the cargo compartments with taunting coming out the other side.

397. For their birthday an unnamed character receives an all-expenses paid vacation to a remote island. It seems that the giver of the present failed to let them know just how remote the island actually is. The character soon finds themselves face to face with inhabitants that aren't too happy with vacationers in their sacred space.

398. While hunting in the woods an unnamed character gets their foot caught in a bear trap. Through the pain they manage to scream for help and when they hear nearby

footfalls they believe that their pleading has worked. Until they hear the gun click.

399. A group of engineers are working high on a wind turbine when a sudden fire breaks loose. The stairwell is consumed before any of them can reach it. They are then faced with a choice, try to make their way through the flames and potentially burn to death, or jump the 225 feet for what will be a certain death.

400. Many individuals can attest to how annoying it is to be stuck in traffic, especially during rush hour. An unnamed character finds themselves stuck on a busy freeway with bumper to bumper traffic on all lanes. At first it's fairly annoying, but after the fifth hour of being stuck in traffic they know something is seriously wrong.

401. An elderly character has lived on the same land for over sixty years and thus, when developers come knocking they downright refuse. However, rather than try to persuade the old timer with more money the group has another idea; they block the character in their own land, no one can get in or out.

402. While skating on a frozen lake some of the ice breaks, causing a few of the characters to fall beneath the hardened surface. Because of the speed in which the

incident happens, no one quite knows which side is right side up and which side leads further into the icy abyss.

403. After a disfiguring accident an unnamed character decides to start life somewhere new. Within a month of living there the same accident occurs again, then again, and again. It seems that the character cannot escape their fate.

404. Tired of such a cruel world, an unnamed character decides to go deep into the forest to die. Only it seems that they can't. The forest won't let them.

405. A young unnamed character has an imaginary friend that, up until this point, has been quite benevolent. Then one day the "friend" encourages the character to go down into the basement, before locking the child down there.

406. One of the most famous places to visit is the Parisian catacombs, the final resting place for many, hundreds of miles long. Suppose an unnamed character and a group of friends decide to check it out before they get lost deep within its labyrinth.

407. After exploring the woods together a group of characters stumble across a strange looking boulder. As soon as one of them touches it they all experience a collective

blackout. When they come to, one of the characters has gone missing.

408. After visiting a living history type of attraction an unnamed character unwittingly does something to upset the town's populace. They are then hunted by the workers, demanding they make amends for what they have done.

409. An unnamed character stumbles across a strange box while walking home from school. Upon touching the box they have a telepathic sense of what the box wants – to lure more people to the strange object.

410. After abandoning their tour guide a group of characters stumble across an old set of ruins deep within the Mexican mountainside. They cannot keep from touching whatever objects they find and soon they are picked off one by one.

Other Phobias

Counting out the full list of phobias may be nearly impossible as any anxiety disorder targeted around a specific fear may be considered a phobia of some sort. There is even phobiaphobia, the fear of fear itself. Many popular works of horror will take these phobias, from the most common to the most unheard of, and utilize them as a vital element to the story. In these prompts we will deal with the following phobias:

- **Coulrophobia:** fear of clowns.

- **Automatonophobia:** fear of humanoid figures.
- **Gerontophobia:** fear of the elderly.
- **Necrophobia:** fear of death or the dead.
- **Trypophobia:** fear of holes, particularly irregular patterns.

Feel free to explore other phobias outside of this list to include in other narratives or to further explore primal fears.

411. Showman's Rest is a real place in the United States that is a mass grave honoring the workers and performers that were killed in the Hammond Circus Train Wreck. This incident happened when another train ploughed into the circus train, killing a total of 86 individuals. Of this number only 56 were buried in the plot, likely due to the lack of family or the inability to identify the bodies; many of which were burned beyond recognition. The gravestones bear such titles as "Unnamed Female" or stage names like "Baldy", "Smiley," or "4 Horse Driver." Craft a scenario in which, on the eve of their deaths, these hapless souls claw their way out of the grave. The real question is – are they looking for revenge or simply miss the limelight?

412. For several nights now a group of clowns have been harassing anyone who chances down the suburbs at night. At first, this is merely annoying, but then all of the bodies begin to show up.

413. A small child is terrified of clowns, but in spite of that they are sent to a cousin's birthday party where "Happy Hands" is set to perform. As it turns out, this child is the only one who can see Happy's monstrous true form.

414. A clown performer has been having trouble securing gigs because of the rampant clown fear affecting locales. So far he has been able to at least secure some regular clients but when they finally bail out he decides to seek bloody revenge.

415. John Wayne Gacy has, unfortunately, become synonymous with the word clown. Envision a scenario, however, in which another will soon take the title of being the most evil clown that ever lived.

416. A young unnamed character is sleeping soundly when they are awoken by the sound of a tinkling bell outside of their window. Upon waking they see a clown who wants nothing more than to lure them away from the safety of their home.

417. In a similar scenario, suppose that it's a group of children that are lured out of homes by a piped piper that relies on face paint and a bag full of tricks.

418. An unnamed character has recently been hired at a small carnival. They are told that everyone there is more than meets the eye but assume it's just a reference to them being good performers. Then one day the character walks in on a group of clowns with their jaws unhinged and the feet of children sliding down their throats.

419. A group of scientists develop a robot with A.I. for the first time. It is not only extremely lifelike, but also aware of every act of sadism enacted upon them by the workers and decides to seek revenge.

420. In a wild attempt to get over their loss, an unnamed character builds a silicone replica of their loved one. Then one night it comes to life, looking exactly like their loved one but emulating a monster.

421. An unnamed character is a reporter at the local news station and is on assignment to interview the head of a robotics company. Everything seems to be going well until there is screaming coming from a nearby room. The lights then flicker and the reporter is outright told this is the end.

422. While walking home from school one day an unnamed character sees a strange doll in a store window. What is

the most unusual about this doll, aside from their eerie lifelike eyes, is that it looks exactly like the character.

423. Since its purchase, a small child has been whispering complaints and fears to their new favorite doll as a coping mechanism. It isn't long before the doll itself becomes sentient and vows to get revenge on all who wrong their owner.

424. After taking a night shift at a department store in the mall an unnamed character decides to have a little fun and put some of the mannequins in compromising positions. They don't seem to like that. Not at all.

425. An unnamed character has just gotten a new roommate. Everything is going well except their roomie has a strange collection of porcelain dolls. Whenever the character passes by them they swear they hear whispering.

426. An unnamed character could never pass up a good deal. Thus, when they see an antique doll at the flea market they ignore the ominous warning from the seller and purchase. By night-time they regret their decision.

427. While on vacation, an unnamed character picks up a strange doll as a gift for their younger sibling. Within a

week the sibling begins to have horrifying nightmares. Within two weeks, the sibling has gone missing.

428. After feeling sorry for an elderly individual sitting alone in the park an unnamed character invites them out to lunch, then later out to dinner. Eventually the two form a friendship and the character invites them over to their place. That's when things really get disturbing.

429. A scientist is so perturbed by their parent's inevitable death that they spend all of their time trying to thwart the aging process. Eventually they do, only to discover too late that some things aren't meant to last forever.

430. After being moved to a new wing in a hospital, an unnamed character is placed next to an elderly patient that can't seem to be quiet. The elderly patient makes loud body noises, talks to themselves, and shouts at all hours of the night. Not being able to take it any longer the character snaps and kills the poor sap. Only later do they find out that they were in the room alone the whole time.

431. After being cursed because of a wrong doing that they have committed, an unnamed character finds that they are suddenly aging very rapidly. If they do not find a way to stop the curse there is no doubt that they will die of natural causes within the week.

432. In a similar scenario, suppose that a character wakes up from a coma that has essentially lasted the entirety of their life. They went in when they were a teenager and they have come out when they are well into their eighties.

433. An elderly character is so lonely that they decide to take out an ad on a local newspaper. Rather than outright seeking friends, or perhaps even a new relationship, the character instead lists their own number as a toll free number. A suicide hotline.

434. After their parents' unexpected death an unnamed character has inherited the care of their grandparent. At first they try their best to honor what their parents would have wanted, but their grandparents behaviour becomes increasingly odd and even downright scary at times.

435. An unnamed character is used to their elderly neighbor's singing. It's sweet, melodic, and even though it happens every night, no one seems to mind the neighbor enjoying their own front porch. When the singing doesn't stop by morning like it usually does the character goes to check it out, only to horrifically discover the neighbor's corpse is still carrying on a haunting tune.

436. All across the world the dead begin to rise from their grave. However, contrary to what many pop culture platforms might say, the dead have no interest in eating the living, but rather they want to give their loved ones a warning about the afterlife.

437. While staying at a moderately priced hotel a young couple can't get over the disgusting smell that seems to have saturated even the bedding of the room. Looking around they finally find a small stain coming down from one of the vents. Inspecting further they find a decaying corpse.

438. During a burial ceremony a corpse is supposed to receive a parting blessing before they go to their final resting place. However, once the priest places a bare hand on the corpse, they instantly become skeletonized and the corpse becomes a living, breathing person again. This is not the first time this has happened.

439. "Coffin birth" refers to the horrific reality in which a deceased mother, because of the build-up of gases inside her body, will push out an often deceased child through her birthing canal. It's quite the grotesque picture. However, picture a scenario in which a character discovers this is how they were born. Sort of. They weren't exactly ever alive.

440. In a feat of scientific wonder, murder victims can be brought to life, only to appear at trial for a very limited time. During one such instance an unnamed character is blamed even though they have never met the victim before in their life.

441. An unnamed character is a body collector, making their money by selling corpses to local medical institutions. One day they go too far and the dead themselves will seek revenge.

442. After making renovations on the house, a young couple find over twenty bodies underneath the floorboard. Rather than alerting the authorities they decide to do something far more sinister instead.

443. While manning a haunted house an unnamed character comes across a prop skeleton that doesn't turn out to be a prop at all. It's real.

444. A morgue worker is all alone with the deceased for the first time after their training. They expect to be pranked in some way, but not like this. The corpse gets up and begins walking around. No one else is inside the building.

445. During a particularly haunting lightening storm a group of drunk friends are on the rooftop of their favorite bar,

watching the display in awe. One of them spots something quite strange in the distance; hundreds of corpses rising from their graves.

446.   After visiting a doctor for a routine check-up an unnamed character gets blood drawn, but the nurse can't seem to find their vein. They are poked once, then again, and again. By the sixth time, the needle is sticking out of their neck and the nurse still can't find any veins.

447.   An unnamed character gets a rash after inadvertently touching a strange plant. At first the spot only itches, but an hour later the first hole appears on their skin.

448.   While out for a job an unnamed character jumps to avoid an ill-placed hole in the ground. Then another appears followed by another. Soon the character is hopping madly trying to avoid all of the holes that have appeared over the surface of the earth.

449.   Craft a scenario in which an unnamed character suddenly finds themselves falling into a sink hole. Since they have managed to survive, if only barely, what might be lurking underneath the Earth's surface.

450.   After receiving a tongue piercing an unnamed character wakes up to find that the piercing has fallen out and there

is a gaping hole in the middle of their tongue. If that wasn't bad enough it seems smaller holes are starting to appear.

451. Suffering from trypophobia an unnamed character visits a mental health professional who tries to get them to understand that the holes they envision all over their body aren't real; it's all in their head. Just when the character finally believes the good doctor, the first *real* hole appears.

452. While routinely cleaning their floor an unnamed character discovers a strange hole that seems to appear out of the blue. They try to cover it up with some extra linoleum, but another hole appears, then another. If this were not startlingly enough, a voice begins to call from the first hole.

453. An unnamed character is something of a thrill seeker and decides to bungee jump into a dark cavern. They suspect they'll reach close to the bottom, have their buddy pull up the rope, and try it all over again until they tire of the sport. The only problem? There is no bottom and the rope seems to be magically infinite.

Monsters, Creatures, & Creepy Crawlies.

Although we will deal with the more classic and human-derived monster in another section, this one deals specifically with monsters that are not and have never been human. In many cases, these creatures may not even look human. Monsters as a horror theme goes back to the earliest known civilizations. The fear stems from the reality that some animals and plants can be deadly to humans, and that fact holds true even in modern times. In addition, there is also the overwhelming fear surrounding the creatures that may not even exist. When you deal with monsters and horror, imagination is key. Whether dealing with an invented monster or an old favorite, it's important to bring something new to the table, especially drawing off the things that scares you the most.

Aliens

Personally, I find otherworldly visitors downright terrifying. If you've read my sci-fi prompt book you know that this theme is often found in science fiction. However, aliens also lend themselves easily to the horror genre as well. When using them as a catalyst for fear the key is not make them front and center. In fact, the most horrifying pieces, whether in film or in literature, uses their presence sparingly. Instead, the fear is centered on the unknown – what do they want? Why are they here? More importantly – what are they going to do us?

454. When the dogs whines to be let out, the unnamed character thinks nothing of it and opens the backdoor. However, the dog doesn't do its business but instead takes off towards the bushes outside. Calling the dog back, the unnamed character decides to go in after it, until they see a figure slinking back, metallic eyes staring out through the shadows.

455. After the government outright says that invasion of Earth has been confirmed, populations all over the world begin to panic. Mass hysteria ensues. This is exactly what the aliens want.

456. The young child sees a stranger wearing a funny black wide brimmed hat and a long overcoat in the middle of summer. The child reaches up and yanks off the hat with a giggle, only to scream in terror at the face before them.

457. An unnamed character wakes up on an operating table with a large, intense light above them. They immediately begin to panic, thinking they must have awoken in an

emergency surgery. They are right. Sort of. Except the doctors aren't exactly human.

458. Suppose that a similar surgery has occurred, but the character is not aware of it until years later. When that happens they have flashes of memory of what has happened and discover a thin scar just behind the nape of their neck.

459. In an apocalyptic world, some of the last remaining humans fight each other over the last bit of resources. The "ending of the world" as many are calling it are because of an aggressive alien race.

460. Suppose that aliens have been using humans for centuries as a type of renewable resource. They take only enough humans so that there is only small murmurings of strange disappearances, but not enough to where it's really noticeable. All of that changes when they need an abundance of resources, and fast.

461. There is an actual belief that the government has made a pact with alien lifeforms. In exchange for allowing the government to test on alien species we have to let them test on some of our populace. Suppose one day this goes horribly wrong when the aliens get a little too greedy. Or, vice versa.

462. Everyone in the office has gone home for the night, leaving an unnamed character alone in a large, high rise. Outside of their window, against the backdrop of the cityscape, they see a monolith of an aircraft gliding past.

463. After a restless night sleep an unnamed character gets out of bed for a glass of water, only to hear the sound of dragging outside. Against their better judgement, they investigate the scene only to find a beloved pet being drug away by a strange humanoid creature.

464. "When did the dreams begin?" The question is asked over and over again. The unnamed character is tired of repeating the answer, but with each session they feel they are one step closer to knowing whether the dreams are just that, or aliens are truly visiting them.

465. A group of hostile aliens target one particular family, aggressively driving them insane. Although much of the horror lies in what they do, a more prominent question might be "why them?"

466. A young unnamed character cries relentlessly about the "bald man in the closet." Their parents try to do as much as they can to quell the child's fears, such as look in the closet themselves, but still every night ends with the

character in tears. Then the parents decide to set up a camcorder, only to catch the alien slipping in the closet while the child sleeps.

467.   One of the most significant aspect of aliens as a monster trope rests in the question of "why are they here?" Some believe that the answer lies in the desire to further explore the universe, while others believe that aliens will only come if they themselves run out of resources. Spin all of these theories on their head and create something new, yet horrifying, instead.

468.   In a similar scenario, suppose the aliens come for a singular person, rather than in terms of the macro. The individual clearly did something to offend the otherworldly beings such as give up coordinates, steal an important object, or so forth. What might happen if no one believes this poor sap?

469.   On a space station hundreds of miles away from Earth all systems are down and a lone astronaut runs the risk of hypothermia. Little do they know that the attack has been caused by aliens outside the vessel.

470.   From birth, an alien species has been keeping track of a human for their own nefarious purposes. When the child comes of age they are now ready for harvesting.

471. While visiting a new building for the first time an unnamed character has to use the restroom. They are told it is in one corner of the building and upon arrival they realize that no one else is there. Thinking they can do their business in private they visit the stall only to see a strange alien creature crawling around on the ceiling above them.

472. A stranded alien seeks the help of an unnamed character in order to get back home. At first the human is more than happy to help and is flattered they have been chosen, but when the alien's behavior becomes more and more bizarre the character tries to back out, but by then it's already too late.

473. The human race has successfully captured a real, living alien. However, there is a mistake at the facility where it is kept and the alien inadvertently goes free. The alien is benevolent, except for those who have wronged it. To those individuals, the alien is extremely cruel in their punishment.

474. An alien species is beginning to die off due to a mutation in their DNA that halts or severely limits reproduction. At first it was manageable, but now it seems almost every new member of the population has this mutation. In

order to prevent the species from dying out entirely aliens must breed with humans. Whether or not these "lower" forms called humans are aware it's even happening to them.

475. To piggy back on the previous scenario, suppose a human has become pregnant with an alien baby and only realizes it after their human looking child begins to exhibit some very odd, and at times, very horrifying behaviors.

476. After thousands of years of speculation, humans finally make first contact with an alien species. It's not a pleasant scenario. Now that the humans have unwittingly made their location known, the alien race can now launch an all-out assault.

477. Suppose first contact is made by a child. The young unnamed character is playing around on the new ham radio they got and a sinister voice makes itself known.

478. Aliens are often known for performing experiments on humans before returning them back to the comfort of their own homes. Why do these operations always go so well? Envision a scenario in which a human is returned in a horrifying and macabre state.

479. An alien is found and discovered by a human. Immediately the creature is rounded up and experimented on within the week. In this scenario, take the POV of the alien and the horror that might occur when the tables are turned.

480. Many stories deal with aliens that have arrived on Earth. This time an astronaut has landed on an alien planet without any means to return home. The world itself is dark, desolate, and the alien creatures here are monstrous creatures with very little intelligence.

481. In the mirror an unnamed character begins to pull off pieces of its flesh, its human suit being cast by the wayside. In the morning they will have regenerated an entirely new form; the humans they are studying none-the-wiser.

482. Craft a scenario in which aliens try humans for the very first time; believing their meat might be palatable. Their theory proves to be correct and humans are soon considered a delicacy.

483. The world's governments have known about the aggressive alien species for quite some time. Since their technology was inferior, the leaders of the world decided it was best to ignore the problem. But now the aliens have

begun to harness new technology that could potentially wipe out millions if not billions.

484. An alien species is parasitic in nature, needing the bodies of others to live. Humans have been chosen for their longer lifespans and how hard it is to detect when one is host to an otherworldly invader.

485. For thousands of years humans have become advanced enough to travel the stars. With that technology they have destroyed thousands of aliens of species. That is until they come across a species that is essentially immortal.

486. After a jog through the neighborhood an unnamed character hears the sound of a child screaming. Instinct takes over and they rush over only to find the child being ripped apart by a group of strange, otherworldly beings.

487. Throughout the life of an unnamed character they have always dreamed of exploring the stars. They get that chance when an alien being brutally rips them from their home and everything they've ever known.

488. Aliens have begun to provide humans with new technology, limitless resources, and other provisions that allow them to gain trust. It is only a setup however and the

reality is that the humans are being groomed for a sinister purpose.

489.   An alien trapped in a cell has been poked, prodded, and has undergone all manners of experimentation. At first glance it seems that the alien simply has a high pain tolerance, but very soon do scientists discover the pain is only making it stronger.

490.   In many alien narratives these otherworldly beings often look very similar to humans in appearance. This often plays on our own ideas that a species more intelligent than us must resemble us in some way. Craft a scenario in which this isn't the case at all. The aliens instead look nothing like humans at all and the fear is intensified because of it.

Animals & Plants

Humans, animals, and plants all have a very complex relationship. Humans eat or use animals and plants, but they can also have animals for pets and can be fully invested into the care and upkeep of a plant when it's in their possession. Every once in a while, that relationship becomes that much more complex when these species decide to fight back.

491.   It started with a scratch on the hand of a small child. The cat in question was, unfortunately, put down for fear of some type of disease. The parents of the child think

nothing of it until news reports start to break out all over the world. Crazed felines begin to attack human in droves. At first the situation seems almost laughable, until big cats join in the assault against the humans.

492. For quite some time a farmer has been bullying some of the outsiders that travel through the village. Little do they know these travellers are magically inclined. On one especially foggy morning the farmer wakes up as a pig. And it's time for the slaughter.

493. Craft a scenario in which the family pet begins to act very strangely, first displaying aggressive stances, but never outright hurting anyone. Then first blood is drawn. Just what is going on?

494. In a similar scenario, suppose the entirety of the world's animals begin to act extremely aggressively towards humans. It isn't with any other species, only the humans. This includes using humans as the only form of sustenance as well.

495. During a late night shift at a pound, an unnamed character is put in charge of euthanizing the animals. They are working later than usual, shoving around, removing and discarding the day's animal corpses;

conscience clear and unbothered – until one of the furry corpses moves.

496. A mentally unstable character grows tired of the neighbor dog's incessant barking. Taking it up themselves they kill the dog and chop the poor animal in tiny little pieces. On a dark, rainy night, the character drives out of town to bury the body. While driving, they hear a barking and banging noise coming from inside the trunk.

497. An unnamed character finds the most adorable kitten they have ever seen. However, every time someone is left alone with the kitten they inexplicably die.

498. Since this section of prompts deals with animals, craft a narrative from the perspective of one. Spin a terrifying yarn from the perspective of an animal that is being chased by a hunter.

499. One strange night an animal rescue volunteer gets an anonymous call to an abandoned animal pound. Thinking the situation odd, the character still walks into the desolate building. Behind them the door clicks shut and ghastly howls and snarls ring out. There's not a living soul inside the building.

500. One of the most horrific real experiments to have taken place is that of the 1950s dog head transplants by Vladimir Demikhov in which one dog's disembodied head was attached to the neck of another. Sadly, this had a 100% mortality rate for the poor canines. But, what if it didn't? What if one such two headed creature survived and is now seeking revenge?

501. An unnamed character accidentally hits a dog on their way home from work. Horrified they try to revive it as best as they can, but it's to no avail. They decide to "do the right thing" and bury the dog on the side of the road. A few nights later the dog's corpse shows up at their front door with a note attached.

502. After a circus performance goes awry an elephant becomes mad and begins to attack the crowd, throwing people around as if they were ragdolls. The elephant begins to target one individual and after tripping, the unnamed characters finds themselves with a large foot placed precariously over their head. Should the elephant step down, the character will be crushed.

503. While on vacation, a wealthy investor continues to come across odd occurrences surrounding the local plant and animal population. Could it be possibly related to the recent harm done to local South American forests or has

something else driven the local wildlife and plant population mad?

504.   After running low on resources, but wanting to remain open, a popular zoo decides to cut corners by feeding the animals a strange mixture. It contains the remains of city strays, curtsey of the local pound. This creates negative consequences in a big way.

505.   During a heavy rainstorm an unnamed character pulls over to the side of the road so they can get their bearings. As soon as the car rolls to a stop a pack of wolves rush the car, snapping, snarling, and trying to tip it over. By the time the character can react and turn the car back on, one of the wolves has already ripped apart a tire.

506.   For years an unnamed character has been involved in a ruthless dog fighting ring. One night the character is roughly taken into a van and soon finds themselves in an abandoned warehouse. When the blindfold is removed they find themselves inside a cage with snarling and snapping dogs being let into it.

507.   Squirrels run rampant on many different college campuses, parks, nature trails, and essentially anywhere a vast amount of humans will migrate. It isn't uncommon for a person to receive a shake down for a potential snack.

However, legends begin to emerge about one such piebald squirrel who will go to any length to get its next meal. Even dangerous ones.

508. When business begins to slow for a taxidermist, they begin to outright kill animals to find more pieces to sell. After stuffing and mounting a particularly beautiful bobcat it beings to let out a terrifying yowl. Other animals follow suit.

509. An unnamed character opens their door one day to find a friendly little parrot on their doorstep. Without context the parrot cries, "You better run. They're coming for you! Awk! They're coming for you! Awk!" The character thinks the display is so funny they let the bird in and soon the parrot becomes their pet. Then one night, the bird flies to the character's bed, leans in their ear and whispers, "They're here."

510. One night an unnamed character is awoken by the distinct sound of howling. The character tries to ignore it, but the sound is so mournful that they decide to investigate. Once outside the character is greeted by several dogs, watching over the recently slain body of the character's loved one.

511. While on a vacation to the Serengeti a foolish traveller decides they will have more photo opportunities if they

walk a little ways away from the vehicle. Before they realize the gravity of their mistake they are surrounded by several hungry lions.

512.   A zoo worker is told by superiors that the newest zoo attraction will be "one for the papers." Not thinking much of being assigned to clean out the cage for the newest animal, the worker hops to it, only to find they are locked in when their job is done. Just then a large and menacing bear is released. Amongst the worker's screams the zoo goers peer through the glass in excitement, a glint of bloodthirstiness evident in everyone's eyes.

513.   While eating a delicious salad an unnamed character suddenly chokes on some dark leafy greens. The food won't come back up and it won't go down. In fact, it's almost as if there is movement inside their throat from something that doesn't want to be eaten at all.

514.   A botanist's experiment to make plants more responsive to humans backfires when one of the plants they are working on begins to develop incisors, limbs, and a taste for flesh.

515.   One morning an unnamed character finds that every room in their house is pitch black due to the windows being blocked. When they open the front door to see what

is going on, they find that too is blocked. As it turns out, their house is in the middle of a strange plant that has swallowed it whole in the middle of the night. It is quite fascinating at first, until several days go by and there is no more food to be found.

516. A scientist attempts to advance the human race by withdrawing the DNA from different animals. Each attempt is just as unsuccessful as the last. On a whim the scientist decides to try plant DNA. It works. Maybe a little too well.

517. An unnamed character finds a strange and unusual plant in a foreign country. Very quickly they learn that the flower's scent can cause anyone to do anything. The character quickly takes the plant back with them, hoping to harness its powers for themselves. This backfires when the plant sprays the character in defence.

518. Plants are sedentary species that are rooted to the spot. How much would change if this were not the case? Would humans still be the dominate species if giant redwoods could walk around or a Venus flytrap might have an easier time choosing its next meal?

519. A mandrake is often believed to have medicinal properties; especially when it comes to motherhood and

fertility. Suppose a character pulls up such a root and hears a sharp scream. This mandrake isn't just a root, but a homunculus.

520. While rummaging around in their garden an unnamed character finds a collection of wildflowers that were not there before. Due to their beautiful and vibrant colors, as well as the placement, the character leaves them alone. However, the next day more flowers appear then more and more until they take over the entire garden. Trying to shear them will not work. Their hardened stalks breaks the steel of the blade.

521. "Stop and smell the roses." It's a statement that gives a reminder of the simple pleasures in life. That is until one strange, carnivorous rose species is discovered. Whenever a human nostril is placed next to the sacred petals, the plant has very powerful, very sharp, and very painful thorns that shoot out.

522. A hapless employee is asked to water their friend's plants while they are on vacation. They are told explicably that these plants can only receive "special" water from the blue container inside the fridge. When the character pours out the liquid substance it comes out red.

523.   Humankind has been extremely lucky in that even one of the world's largest carnivorous plants, tropical pitcher plants, will only eat rodents and lizards. Envision a scenario in which a new, and very large, plant is discovered that has the ability to digest human meat and has already begun to act on that ability.

524.   While sleeping peacefully in bed an unnamed character suddenly rouses from their slumber and has a hard time trying to move their arm, then a leg, and so forth. It turns out thick vines have wound themselves around the character's entire frame. If the vines keep growing the character won't be able to breathe.

525.   An unnamed character is enjoying tea with a relative when suddenly they begin seizing up and having convulsions. Within minutes they are dead. This begins to happen the world over, but only those that use a certain type of tea leaf.

526.   Deep in the forest, an unnamed character hears the sound of crackling. The sound is similar to logs in a fire. The further they walk, they louder the noise gets. Finally they come across rows upon rows of giant carnivorous plants. A human leg is sticking out of one of them. The sounds are people being digested whole.

527.   The entire day, an unnamed character has been randomly hearing, "Beware the Red Lily" from various people. The landlady said it upon leaving, it was in the header of an email, the barista wrote it on the character's cup, and a street preacher yelled it when they passed by. Upon returning home, the character finds a red lily on the kitchen counter.

Small Creatures

Despite being much larger than many creatures, humans still have an innate fear of anything perceived threatening. For instance, Entomophobia or insectophobia is the fear of bugs, while murophobia is the fear of rats. What is it about roaches, spiders, rodents, lizards, or any other kind of creepy crawling creature that alarms us so? Perhaps it is in the nature of the swarm itself, uncontrollable and wild. Small creatures have a unique place in the annals of horror, often used as a jump scare or simply adding to the ambience. Here, they are the focus.

528.   An unnamed character gets up in the middle of the night to get themselves a little midnight snack. While traversing the length of the hallway they get a sharp pain in their foot, then another and another. Hopping on one foot they make their way to a nearby chair and flop into it after switching on the lights. In horror, they see gaping holes that spurt out with their own blood. The skin twitches and pulls back as the head of little black creatures emerge.

529. An unnamed character is digging in their garden when little bugs start to surface. At first it's nothing more than a little annoying, but then they find these creatures can jump and bite. Hard.

530. A young character picks beautiful flowers that they find near their home. When they bring the flowers inside a small collection of insects crawl out and make a beeline straight for the ears of anyone who touches the gorgeous plants.

531. While relaxing in their living room a fly buzzes around until landing on an unnamed character's leg. After the character kills the fly, another fly lands and the character kills it as well. Two more flies land on the character's legs. The character kills them. More and more flies land on the character, until they weigh them down. Flies begin to spill from the cracks in the windows and through the vents.

532. Many individuals are deeply scared of roaches. Some not only detest the sight of them, but will also scream loudly whenever one is nearby. In this scenario, give the characters a real reason to be afraid. Not only is there an infestation, but these roaches don't wait for a body to rot before they dig in.

533. A reality competition goes awry when an unnamed character is lowered into a coffin and hundreds of bugs are dumped on top of them. There is so many bugs, and so many cheers, that no one seems to notice that the character has begun screaming.

534. To piggyback on the above scenario, suppose the designated time has now passed and the character can be let out of the coffin. However, when the bugs are cleared away only skeletal remains are left. What kind of impact might this have on the other contestants? Especially if the show must go on.

535. After vacationing, an unnamed character returns back home with strange bumps all over their body. They are itchy, but not painful and the character thinks nothing of it. Until worms begin to emerge several days later.

536. While enjoying a delicious snack, an unnamed character bites down on something extremely crunchy. The only problem? They are eating plain yogurt. In this scenario, the food item can of course be replaced with anything that should not crunch.

537. An unnamed character kills an insect without thought, simply wanting to remove it from their home. Sometime later the character kills another, and then another. They

can't be certain, but it seems very much like it's the same one.

538.   Craft a narrative that deals with the world on a micro level. In this scenario take the point of view of a lone insect and how frightening the world must be like when every second is a battle for survival.

539.   An entomologist discovers a rare breed of insect that is not only capable of intelligent thought, but is a warring species that has its sights set on humans.

540.   While walking home from school after a heavy rainstorm a young character takes a detour to play with some of the worms that have washed up. Little do they know, one of the worms has crawled into a cut on the child's leg.

541.   While playing truth or dare an unnamed character decides to be brave and accept whatever outlandish stunt is thrown their way. "Eat a bug!" Not wanting to play the fool the character finds a bug and then swallows it in one pained gulp. It isn't until later at the party do they realize the bug is still alive inside of them.

542.   There are many extreme types of tortures. In this scenario envision a scene in which an individual is taken and put into a large 6ft by 6ft box. Although they cannot see

anything, they can certainly feel creatures crawling around from head to foot.

543. An unnamed character is stranded on an island far away from civilization. They are close to starving and their only method of survival is to eat strange bug-like creatures. They've never seen anything like these tiny insects before and they don't know if they are poisonous or not. However, with no plants or other potential edible offerings on the island it may be their only choice.

544. A couple is enjoying a nice, relaxing moment outside on the balcony of their hotel room. They have saved quite a while for this and they are going to enjoy every moment. Soon they hear the sound of thousands of beating wings. In the distance a collection of large flying insects are headed straight for them. Instinctively, they move to head back inside. Only the door is locked.

545. A young child wakes up from a nightmare in which they are attacked by a humanoid figure made entirely of insects. They scream for their parent, who instantly responds. Outside the door they hear their parent's voice, but also the sound of tiny objects falling to the ground with each footstep.

546.   After a few days of settling in to their new house an unnamed character finally sets up some of the appliances and makes them a piece of toast. Out pops a wiggling, disgusting roach. Then a few more crawl out. Horrified, the new owner throws the toaster away only to find the same problem with the blow dryer, TV, and every other electronic that is used.

547.   An unnamed character is enjoying a nice, relaxing nature hike when they see a strange black river just ahead. Curiously, they go to investigate only to realize that it isn't a river at all. It's a vast collection of ants. Additionally, they know these might be monstrous ants by the skeletons they leave behind.

548.   Many are familiar with olden day prison cells in which the accused were chained to a wall. Envision a scenario in which a prisoner hears scuttling paws in the distance and no matter how hard they struggle in their shackles, they know that they might soon be food for hungry rats.

549.   A scientist is hard at work in their gene-splicing lab, hoping to use various small rodents to cure the many diseases that plague the world. Human ears are attached to the backs of rabbits, the bubonic plague is given freely to rats, and so on. What the scientist didn't count on is the

fact that the animals were not only growing intelligently, but their desire for vengeance is growing as well.

550.   A rat king is a large collection of rodents, generally dead, whose tails are tied together because of feces, glue, or another unfortunate occurrence. Suppose a character stumbles across a rat king in which the rats are not only alive, but working together against your character despite their predicament.

551.   Sleepily, an unnamed character wakes up in the middle of the night to the sound of muffled voices. Living in an apartment they think nothing of it until they hear the sound of pattering feet from inside the walls as well. The voices don't seem entirely human. If so, what on earth could they be?

552.   While working on a pipeline, an engineer finds a strange blob-like substance. Although it is inky black in color, it isn't anything like an oil drop. The engineer leans down to get a better look. Unfortunately, that is the worst thing that they could have done.

553.   Dozens and dozens of rodents have been set forth when an unnamed character goes urban exploring in an abandoned ranch. Thankfully, they have got a pistol with

them, only this is no protection against the gnashing creatures that seem impervious to bullets.

554. An unnamed character has been warned, several times, about letting their trash fester outside their door. The character hasn't had a reason to listen to their landlords, that is, until strange creatures begin to emerge from the mountain of rubbish.

555. An unnamed character is paralyzed after they take a tumble down the side of a mountain. Not only is their situation made difficult by the fact they can't move and can barely cry for help, but they seemed to have landed on a very large anthill as well.

556. An unnamed character is extremely excited to receive the latest smartphone in the mail. What they don't realize is that a brain-eating bug is lying dormant in the phone's interior. The character will learn this fact the minute they place the phone to their ear.

557. There are thousands of them. Small, ugly creatures surrounding a young unnamed character going for a dip in the family pool. The more they struggle the closer the creatures come. Just how will this character make it out of this predicament alive?

558. Daylight has always been associated with good omens, while night time with bad. Spin that ideology on its head. Suppose there is a place in which ravenous, flesh eating creatures will come out only when the sun is at its brightest.

559. As part of a ritual a shaman is supposed to eat live bugs, which is not only done for show, but to also better con people into thinking the shaman has magical abilities. Normally, the shaman shows his tongue, indicating the last bug has been eaten, and patrons pay up. This time the shaman falls over dead and their bare stomach begins to undulate strangely.

560. Death comes to us all. Of this we are certain. But, what happens after we die? An unnamed character has been dead for a few days now, but miraculously comes back to life, still in the place where they were left unfound. Unfortunately, not only was no one aware that they passed, but grave worms and other creepy crawlies are still keen on continuing with their feast.

561. Most artists are aware of the small wooden figure that helps with anatomy. Suppose in the dead of night that figure comes to life. The narrative you craft would be

equally effective with any other small figurine that you can think of (e.g. ceramic figure, small toy, puppet, etc.)

562. The movie *Toy Story* is one of the most popular children's franchises of all times. Most of its desirability rests on the love the toys have for the kids that play with them. Craft a narrative that deals with the opposite. Toys that have a downright disdain for children.

563. An unnamed character has had trouble sleeping for quite some time. Finally, they pinpoint the issue and place the blame on a lumpy mattress. They pull back the sheets to try and make adjustments, but instantly break into a gut wrenching scream. Just what is it that they see?

Giant Monsters

The subgenre of monster horror fiction is very popular in Asian culture and especially in 1950s B-horror movies. Most are familiar with King Kong, Godzilla, and countless other giant insect or people that are the result of some form of radiation. More recently, the popular manga and anime series, *Shingeki no Kyojin* or *Attack on Titan* has once more relied on the giant monster trope to strike fear in the hearts of viewers. Like with the concept of small creatures, this section relies on inventing these large scale monsters, with plenty of inspiration drawn from real life monoliths.

564. While studying the Mariana Trench in a submarine, a group of scientists stare out the porthole, looking at the curious species of fish swimming by. Then, without warning, a large tentacle sweeps by. Although giant squid are common this far below the water's surface, this tentacle is just a little bit different – it ends in what can only be presumed to be fingers.

565. An oil spill causes an octopus to mutate into a larger, more terrifying creature. Before the crew can send for backup the octopus begins to reach in and grab the crew one by one.

566. Envision a scenario in which an insect, particularly a disgusting or dangerous one, has grown to the size of an elephant. Soon, the insect will grow even larger.

567. After a long day at the office, an unnamed character hopes to relax and watch some TV. They don't get to have a moment to do any of that because on the opposite end of their threshold, taking up much of their wall, is a 6x6 giant roach.

568. A lone sailor finds themselves washed ashore of a seemingly desolate island. While there are no people on this island there certainly are giant whale-sized monsters.

569. Dogs are typically considered "man's best friend." However, although large breeds of dogs are in existence, envision a scenario in which a new breed crops up. One in which a semi-truck would look small by comparison.

570. An unnamed character is jarred awake in the middle of the night. Curiously, they hear the faint sound of tapping from underneath the bed. Reaching out, they are suddenly grabbed by a large writhing tentacle.

571. An unnamed character is proud of their pet tarantula. Oftentimes, they take it out, play with it and then put it back in their enclosure. One morning after taking it out, the character notices the spider has grown. The next day, it's grown a little larger. And so on.

572. In a similar scenario, suppose that the pet is some type of snake. However, this time the growing creature is still loved dearly by the pet owner – that is until too many neighbors are eaten.

573. Bugs. Giant bugs, everywhere! The character wakes up, laughing at themselves for such a silly and strange dream. That's when they hear loud buzzing outside their window.

574. An unnamed character finds a spider inside their home. They get a shoe and slam it down on the creature.

However, instead of dying, another spider pops out. This one is larger than the previous one. When the character hits that spider, *another* spider pops out, much larger than the first two. This happens again and again.

575. A very rich and well to-do unnamed character lives on the top floor of a fancy building in a luxury penthouse. They step out onto the balcony to get a breath of fresh air only to find that the city is in ruins. The large monolith responsible is now headed straight towards them.

576. A hunter is walking down a deep path in the woods. They hear the rustling of leaves and then let out a long scream. A large animal, unlike anything they've ever seen before, is chewing on their partner. They stop mid-bite and run straight towards the hunter.

577. A small child befriends a giant. The giant protects the child and tells them stories about a place where many large humans roam free. In exchange, the child provides them with ample bullies to eat.

578. An investigator studies the crime scene carefully. No murder weapon. No tracks. Whatever did this was big. Very big. And likely not even human.

579. A doctor has an unusual case – a patient that won't stop growing. Although this happens in real life due to various diseases, this time the patient grows several feet per day.

580. An unnamed character is going on a nature hike when they decide to go on a trail they've never been to. There they find that the large pine trees that surround them not only move, but are also sentient.

581. A fisherman hauls in quite the catch – a large fish creature almost the size of the boat itself. Strangely, they soon find out that they've only caught *part* of the creature. The rest is still in the ocean depths. Just how large is this thing?

582. Many cultures have stories of giants. People that are often three sizes bigger than the tallest human. Suppose such a race exists now, but they have developed a particular taste for what they call "the lesser ones."

583. It has finally happened. Aliens have landed from another world. Rather than little green men, these creatures are large, terrifying monsters.

584. Crabs. Thousands of them have washed ashore. Strangely enough, these are extremely large. While the ones on the shoreline are dead, there is still the possibility that more of these monoliths remain in the ocean.

585. On an island, undiscovered, there is a race of giants. Although they are generally a peace-loving breed. All of that will soon change when they are under attack.

586. Thinking on the themes of giants again, craft a scenario in which the skeleton of one is discovered in a rural area. The result causes a panic amongst the town.

587. An unnamed character awakens to find themselves stuck to their own bedroom wall. The entirely of the room is covered with white, almost translucent strands. A spider's web.

588. Centuries ago, there were many wars that broke out, with many different ways in which to secure victory. One such way is through the use of warhorses. Though this time they are large, horrible beasts called nightmares.

589. A painter can't seem to stop drawing giant monsters, each as horrifying as the next. The painter claims these creatures really exist, but they are constantly dismissed as simply having an overactive imagination. That is, until now.

590. While traveling through a desert, an explorer realizes too late that they are lost. They also quickly realize that there are giant sandworms in this desolate place.

591. Most individuals are aware of the Godzilla and giant monster mythos. Create a narrative that doesn't put the monster on land or sea, but rather in the air.

592. Giant creatures have destroyed much of civilization. That is except for a small pocket of survivors. Write a tale that focuses on them even though humanity is doomed to fail.

593. A scientist releases something horrifying into the ocean – a prehistoric shark. The scientist only wanted to gauge the creature's reaction in a natural habitat, but didn't bank on the monster breeding with another shark. Now there are several monstrosities in the ocean.

594. An unnamed character is excited to go to a Jurassic themed park. The animatronics are extremely life-like. Just a little *too* real.

595. Just how big can a giant monster get? Craft a scenario in which you test the limits of what might be possible.

596. Too often we see these horror narratives reflected from perspective of the miniscule humans. What if we instead

saw things from the giant monster point of view? Perhaps it is they who feel threatened.

597. Using a similar ideology craft a scenario in which the monster is actually a giant, not a creature like in the above prompt. The largest human that ever lived. Suppose they still have a taste for human flesh, but the thing is – they feel really, really bad about it.

598. A young unnamed character finds a strange gelatine-like substance on their desk. Very quickly they learn the blob will destroy any object fed to it. At first the character thinks it's fun. Then when the substance grows larger and consumes half the house, the fun is over.

599. An unnamed character goes to sleep one morning with everything relatively normal, but wakes up in a world of giants. The trees, their neighbors, even the family pet is all grotesquely larger. However, everything else has remained relatively the same.

Mythological Foes

Legendary creatures are those that have become staples of mythological lore. Often, they are symbolic in order to represent some kind of belief system or moral code that the culture stands behind. Although these creatures generally factor into the fantasy genre, they can also be used effectively in horror if done correctly.

The key is to not focus on the morality that surrounds them, but rather on what kind of terror or havoc they may cause, which further parallels the established tensions and fear of your particular narrative.

600.   A group of fisherman are chatting aside a nearby pond when one of them lets out a yell and points somewhere in the distance. Alarmed, the others follow their gaze only to see a humanoid creature, roughly the size of a child in the distance. The creature has a flattened-like head covered by a crown of thick shaggy hair. The kappa is a creature that is mischievous in nature. Such as drownings.

601.   In a similar scenario, suppose that a kappa lives near a lake that no one really inhabits, that is until one such character discovers the sinister nature of this dark body water and begins to use the creature for their own evil purpose.

602.   Looking at another watery creature, and a more modern myth, suppose the infamous loch ness monster is not only real but is a known predator. Whether or not the government has been covering its existence up is a moot point, what matters is the vacationers who mysteriously vanish around the water's edge.

603.   In South America, the *Yuca Mama* is said to be a giant (about 120ft, but stories vary) water snake that lives in the

murkiest of rivers. For obvious reasons no one believes these stories until one day a carcass of such a creature is found and inside are the decaying remains of several human corpses.

604. Another African legend, this one hailing from West Africa, speaks of the *Niniki Nanka*, which is a snake-like creature that has also been said to have legs and walk on land. No matter what the appearance, villagers believe that anyone who sees the creature will immediately die soon after. An unnamed character is lucky in that they have survived the sighting, but the real question is – how?

605. Dragons are often cited as one of the most recognizable fantasy creatures of all time. However, how can they fit into the horror genre? For a creature so well-known is it possible to bring fear to the audience with such fantastical expectations?

606. An unnamed character hears deep rasping coming from the bushes at night. At first they think the noise is someone breathing, which is fairly scary in and of itself. Then the truth is made clear; it's a large reptilian creature dragging a body out of view.

607. Throughout history, many mythologies are often centered on a human being turned into an animal after being

punished, usually by the gods. Suppose this is the case for one unnamed character, but they also plan to get revenge on those who cursed them.

608. While walking through the woods one day an unnamed character stumbles across a hurt creature straight out of a fairytale. They attempt to help the creature in any way that they can, only to unfortunately discover that it was just a ruse to fill a hungry belly.

609. An unnamed character goes on a date with someone that is not only attractive, but also seems to be very kind hearted as well. Everything seems to be going swimmingly until the character seeks a kiss and find themselves staring into cold, snake-like eyes. Their date certainly wasn't like that a minute ago!

610. After moving into a new property an unnamed character notices their neighbor has a penchant for collecting strange statues. Perhaps a little more interesting is that each one is posed in odd contorted positions with grimaces etched on their stone faces. Are these even statues at all?

611. A child with many legs is born in a remote village. The locals view the child as a monstrosity while others view the

child as a god of some sort. The truth, however, is much more horrifying.

612. During the middle of a church service many patrons start screaming when a winged creature is found dangling from one of the rafters. It seems something ancient and old has been awakened. In this scenario any type of religious institution can be used.

613. There is a legend that says the first one to be buried in the cemetery will help all others pass to the other side. This is often depicted as a large black dog. Envision a scenario in which the dog shows up at a character's window one chilly night.

614. Thousands of years ago humankind had to battle each other and vicious animals as well. What if they truly also faced horrific mythological creatures? Would history would have been shaped differently?

615. While many have heard of centaurs there are many other types of 'taurs as well. An ichtocentaur, for instance has both the body of a horse and the tail of a fish. Utilize a new 'taur type to craft your horror narrative.

616. The ancient kraken is a squid-like monster that could strike down ships in one fell swoop. A new species of beast

is discovered. They may be the size of chickens, but they are just as vicious.

617.   A cave explorer finds a set of strange and ancient runes splatter across the walls. While this normally wouldn't be horrifying in this case the description warns that an ancient and vengeful beast lies entombed, waiting to be awoken.

618.   Night after night a creature from legend sneaks into a bustling downtown city and steals away a few humans for a late night snack. Just what is this creature and more importantly, how can it be stopped?

619.   Screams ring out in a bustling hospital when a patient suddenly starts to attack nurses and staff. Perhaps even more startlingly is the fact that they have sprouted wings and claws.

620.   An unnamed character stands on top of a summoning stone and visualizes what mythical creature they might bring forth. They are so indecisive that everything backfries and they summon a weird agglomeration of several creatures.

621.   A seasick sailor leans over the side of the boat and proceeds to get sick. Afterwards, a group of angry

merpeople begin to attack the boat demanding retribution for such a slight.

622. A young unnamed character has been swept out to shore. Close to drowning they have been saved by a water nymph. Only they aren't headed in the direction of the shore, but rather further into the water.

623. An unnamed character wakes up trapped in a fantasy world. Rather than run into sweet natured creatures like elves or pixies, they instead meet the most fearsome of all beasts – a unicorn.

624. An unnamed character visits a psychic in a quest to find answers. Before the character receives any kind of world shattering insight, however, they are given several riddles. Turn out they are dealing with a thousand year old sphinx.

625. Two friends are on the front porch when one of them sees something in the thick foliage. It's big and has far too many legs.

626. While out on the trail, a group of hikers sees something strange flying overhead. It has the body of a lion and wings and head of a hawk. The creature would be

considered majestic if it didn't just grab one of the hikers and eviscerate them right there in the sky.

627. Everywhere a character looks are goblins. Thousands of them. The question is not only how did the character get in this predicament, but how will they get out?

628. A young unnamed character receives a box on the front doorstep. Their parents don't pay any attention until they hear a strange screeching coming from inside.

629. At a flea market an unnamed character purchases a beautiful red bird. For the next few days everything in their life seems to be improving. That is, until their house burns down, the bird included. Amongst the rubble the bird's music can still be heard.

630. After purchasing a new home, an unnamed character walks into the cellar to store some old boxes. What they find is a collection of very angry, and very hungry, harpies.

631. An unnamed character wakes up inside a dark and dank cave. They think it's some kind of joke until a large scaly creature approaches them with fire coming out of its nose.

632. An elderly maid is desperate to keep their job even though they are no longer physically able to handle the workload. They make a pact with a bakru, made of both flesh and wood. The work is done in half the time, but it comes at a price.

633. For several days now an unnamed character has been followed by a woman who says nothing, but screams as loud as she can at exactly noon. The character is unaware that the woman is a banshee, warning the character about their impending death.

634. While relaxing in their apartment, an unnamed character hears loud stomping from the floor upstairs. Finally at their wits end, the character goes to confront the occupant only to realize they are dealing with an annoyed cyclops.

635. Many of us have our own favorite mythos from around the world. Some favor eastern or western narratives while some dive into more local affairs. For this scenario, choose a mythological creature, ideally one of your favorites, and break its surrounding trope. A good example for this would be having the Loch Ness monster be actually a land creature or the sphinx lacking intelligence or riddles. The key is to make it horrifying rather than campy.

636.   A basilisk is a snake-like creature that is said to be able to kill a person with a single glance. Suppose one has just made its way into a very crowded pet store.

637.   An unnamed character falls head over heels for their co-worker. Something about the peer's mischievous charm draws them in. It's too bad the character is dealing with a kitsune.

Neo-Monsters

Neo, or "New" monsters are exactly what they sound like – monsters that have not really been seen before, whether in a classical or modern sense. As a storyteller in the horror genre, it is important to know when to rely on classic tropes and when to bring your own inventiveness to the table. In this case, creating your own monster, or finding a new way to spin an old favorite will really separate your work from what's already out there. Although there are many monsters to draw from, here are some monsters that simply do not fall into a previous category or have only recently been crafted.

638.   It started off as a strange purple gloop that sputtered anytime anyone got near it. It was so nonthreatening, even lying on the edge of a vacant road, that no one noticed when it got bigger. Further still, there was no one around to watch when the gloop swallowed a whole rat that happened to chance near its gelatinous form. Yes, no one saw the bones, skin, and fur digest in the blink of an

eye. It wasn't until the strange gloop was already five feet in stature and three feet wide, and its appetite moving on to small mammals, that anyone took notice. By that the time the military is called in, a few town residents have already gone missing and the gloop is the size of a small house.

639. A writer famous for creating strange and ferocious fictional creature and beasts in their stories is taken back when they come home to find the exact manifestation of one of their earliest creatures, snarling at them from across the room.

640. Craft a fairytale with a horror bent. Rather than having a character face a dragon or other mythical creature, envision a scenario in which they must face a large, horrifying monster of your own design.

641. An unnamed character is driving down a winding road in the middle of the night. In their headlights they can see an outline of a creature. Humanoid in shape the thing seems to blend in with the light. So much so that when the lights go off the creature is gone.

642. While trying out a few wedding gowns a young bride suddenly finds herself constricted to the point where she

cannot breath. It is almost like the clothes are actually alive.

643.   In the snowy tundra a team of explorers come across strange monsters made of ice. They cannot be killed because once destroyed they simply reconfigure with more snow.

644.   An unnamed character works at a call center. A job they absolutely loathe. The pay is terrible, the callers are really mean, and the hours are tough. However, there is soon a silver lining when they discover that there is a creature digitally living in the phone lines. And it loves nothing more than to do that character's bidding.

645.   They call it the hate monster. A being that will outright kill those that would spread hatred. Unfortunately, it has no sides. No way to determine what "hate" actually is. That makes things slightly more complicated.

646.   There are hundreds of holidays a year. Choose one and envision a scenario in which a symbol of this holiday comes to life, such as gingerbread men at Christmas or sugar skulls on *Dia Del Los Muertos*, the Day of the Dead.

647.   After a heavy rainstorm an unnamed character inspects their property to assess the damage. While doing so, their

leg gets stuck in a pile of mud. The more they struggle, the harder it is to get out. It's almost as if the sludge is...*alive*.

648. A powerful CEO goes to the woods to get away from it all after a huge merger fails to go through. When they return they are raving about the creatures that live there. They convince several board members to accompany them on a follow up trip. The CEO is determined to prove that what they saw is true. Is it some type of trap or are there truly monsters in the woods?

649. A group of characters are traveling together during a snowstorm when the car's engine suddenly gives out. They quickly argue with each other about who gets to go outside and check. What they don't realize is that what they should be worried about is already inside the car.

650. A nice family dinner is interrupted by the sounds of scratching on the roof. They quickly assume it's some type of animal and promise to deal with it after they finish their food. However, they shouldn't wait too long because the sounds are not coming from an animal, but something much, much worse.

651. Some of the most terrifying creatures on Earth live in the deepest parts of the ocean. Use one of these animals as inspiration for creating a new monster.

652.	An unnamed character gets new tattoo put on by their favorite artist. The artist asks if the character would like to try some new ink, which is supposed to help with fading. The character agrees and realizes too late that the ink doesn't fade because it comes to life.

653.	The human face is unique and easily recognizable. People have seen it in the condensation of window panes, on the barks of trees, and even on the surface of toast. Place the human face on a place where it doesn't belong, whether it is an inanimate object or an animal.

654.	An unnamed character is taking out the trash at night when they hear a familiar voice whispering to them. They immediately go to investigate only to come across a monster that copies the voice of the last thing that it ate.

655.	An unnamed character has gone to the eye doctors several times in the last few weeks. No matter what, the outcome is always the same. Their eyes are as healthy as ever. But, the patient insists they are seeing visions of monsters. Turns out, they are.

656.	Ah, the unassuming oyster. Many would say that they are delicious while others might only want the pearls they produce. Suppose a group of them are harvested, but they aren't oysters at all, but a strange creature that is using a similar shell in order to chew their victims from the inside out.

657.   It lies in the fire, a strange slithering thing. Most adept at hiding in the fireplace of human homes. This makes it easier to satiate their hunger.

658.   "If you swallow the watermelon seeds, a watermelon will grow inside your stomach." That's the adage that many of us have heard growing up. Of course it's not true. That is, not for watermelon seeds anyway.

659.   While cleaning out their garage, an unnamed character finds a collection of strange, pulsating sacs. Immediately they assume they are eggs from larger-than-normal spiders and set to work clearing them out. They are partly right. They are eggs, just not spider eggs.

660.   Sometimes sacrifices must be made. At least that's what an unnamed character tells themselves. Their goal is to bring forth a monster of their own design.

661.   Most creatures are hideous by design. The scarier the better. Instead, envision a scenario where a monster is incredibly cute and that's exactly what helps it lure in its prey.

662. Suppose there is a monster that can create other monsters. An unnamed character must stop it before the entire world is overrun with these strange creations.

663. Who says that all monsters are bad? Suppose a monster is discovered that can heal any wound. It can potentially cure all the world's ills…at the right price, of course.

664. An unnamed character wakes up with tumors and deformities all over their body. Doctors are baffled until they discover that the culprit is a parasitic creature that attacks on a cellular level.

665. Monsters walk amongst us. Using our form to hide in plain view. Sickeningly enough, they enjoy the taste of human flesh and always have a bit of fun before their victims are consumed whole. The ray of hope comes from the fact that these cretins are easily recognizable due to their grotesquely elongated fingers and toes.

666. A small child wakes up in the middle of the night to the sound of screaming. They look out the window to see hundreds of cackling creatures. Just what are these things and where did they come from?

667. A group of campers are gathered around the campfire telling each other urban legends. Eventually they tire of this game and play "Mary Shelley," where they must split up and create a unique horror monster. Scariest one wins. Soon the creatures they concoct come to life and begin to kill off the others, one-by-one.

668. Snow falls quietly on the ground and an unnamed character comes across an injured creature lying half dead in the forest. It's humanoid and not like anything anyone's ever seen before. The character nurses it back to health before instantly regretting doing so when the monster attacks them first.

669. A young unnamed character has been warned against going into their parent's shed out in the woods. Finally, when their parents are gone and the babysitter falls asleep they seize their chance. What they find downright terrifies them. A collection of caged monsters from all over the world. Some are straight from the child's nightmares.

670. Fireflies. Thousands of them dance across the night sky while an unnamed character walks at midnight. They are beautiful. That is until one lands on their outstretched hand. This isn't a firefly at all. It's a creature that is able to give off its own light from the blood it swallows.

Slashers, Snatchers, & Real Life Crime.

Real life is stranger than fiction, as the saying goes. For any true crime lover, journalist, or even most horror fans themselves, the knowledge of this holds true in many cases. There is just no accounting for the real life horror that members of the human race inflict on one another. Writers who want to delve in this kind of horror should be careful to tread lightly. If your work is just shocking and gruesome enough then you've instilled terror in your audience and your work one of the most talked about pieces because there is ample food for thought. However, cross a certain threshold and you've completely turned your audience off. The problem is, this threshold is different for every person. Thus, as you craft your narrative you must constantly revaluate your work and gauge what you are trying to say and what devices you are utilizing to tell it. Generally, if you use a crime story straight from real life it's no longer a horror story – it's a true crime. Additionally, if you include gore just for the purpose of shock value, you are entering a specific subgenre of horror that only meets a certain audience demand. You will be more adept at understanding these key differences the more you write and the more you evaluate your own work.

Serial Killers

Generally a serial killer is defined as an individual that kills three or more people within a month or two interval. Although there are a lot of different theories as to why serial killers commit atrocious murders in succession – from brain damage to childhood abuse, there is no doubt that some of the most horrific crimes have been committed by them. When serial killers actively hunt their victims it often comes in three different forms:

- Organized: Serial killers methodically plan their kills, often going after specific targets and utilizing specific methodologies.
- Disorganized: Overall lack of a specific modus operandi (M.O.). They do not utilize a specific methodology and may not have specific targets in mind.
- Mixed: These serial killers either switch between organization or disorganization, or they may have an organized method and disorganization in their chosen victims. Sometimes vice versa.

Keep this idea in mind as you create your wave your criminological tale of horror.

671.   After a routine traffic stop an unnamed character is pulled over for a broken taillight. The whole thing should be over in a matter of minutes, but what catches the officer's eye is the skittish way this character is acting. What's worse is that they have a cooler in the backseat despite temperatures being below zero. The officer inquiries about the cooler, but instead of responding the suspect drives off in a panic. Had the officer managed to open they cooler they would understood why – there's a severed head in there.

672.   While out on a walk, an unnamed character finds themselves brutally attacked from behind. They attempt to resist, but before long they find themselves in the back of someone's trunk with air dwindling fast. You can change the scenario by changing the location of abduction or up the fear by already having a corpse in the trunk.

673.   A young character is walking home from school when they sees a woman being dragged into the woods by a masked assailant. The character must then decide whether to follow in an effort to help, knowing they might suffer from the same fate or run and get help, but in doing so could potentially cause the life of the victim.

674. Envision a similar scenario, but rather than have the unnamed character stumble across a crime in progress they instead find a corpse, or worse; the serial killer's entire liar.

675. While poking around an oddity shop an unnamed character finds a great deal on a real human skull. They purchase the strange item and promise to come back the next week. Not only do they keep their word, but they are surprised to find out that the shop has a new skull on display. The process is repeated over and over again. The real question is – where did this bounty of human remains come from?

676. A car is pulled over by a curious cop. No, it isn't their taillights, the speed they are going, or anything of that nature, but rather the strange liquid dripping from the back. When the officer pops open the trunk their worst fears are proven correct.

677. One of the most infamous slayers is Jack the Ripper, whose identity is still a mystery, though highly speculated. Some of the accused include Francis Thompson, Dr. T. Neill Cream, Walter Sickert ,and even Lewis Carroll. In this scenario, envision that an unnamed character knows the true identity of the ripper, but must then decide what to do with it.

678. Suppose that an unnamed character is a serial killer. How might they go about choosing their victims? What is their modus operandi? More importantly, do they have a shred of guilt over the terror they bring?

679. An unnamed character finds themselves locked in a basement chained to a very sturdy pillar. The air smells strongly of death and they are smart enough to know that if they don't get out soon they might just suffer the same fate. Problem is that they can't seem to remember how they got there in the first place.

680. After the town's recluse dies it is up to the government to take over the property. When they begin the search they find the house in complete disarray; from food containers over twenty years old to piles of rat nests. If this wasn't bad enough they also find remains that prove the individual was the slayer the police were hunting for over 40 years.

681. Although the term "serial killer" typically refers only to the slaying of people, craft a scenario in which a slayer goes after beloved pets. Will these crimes be taken seriously and furthermore, how might this mad person be stopped?

682. Envision a scenario in which an unnamed character has been accused of slayings that they did not commit. Perhaps it was even a case of being at the wrong place at the wrong time or bearing an uncanny resemblance to the true murderer. How do they prove their innocence then?

683. Expand on the above scenario. Craft a narrative in which not only is the accused character not only innocent, but suppose they know who the real killer is. Even worse, the real killer knows who they are as well.

684. A serial killer seemingly kills at randomly, their victims are different in age, color, race, and so forth. They have no relation to each other. It all seems so very random until the detectives notice one small fact. The killer is spelling out someone's name.

685. An unnamed character has been brutally attacked by a serial killer but somehow has managed to survive. During their recovery, not only are they still traumatized over what happened to them, but they are terrified by the fact that the killer is still out there and wants to silence them for good.

686. A patient of a hospital is moved into a new wing by accident. In this wing there are mostly individuals who are invalid and unable to care for themselves. On the first

night a doctor comes in and administers something to the patient, who dies shortly after. The next night the same thing happens to a new patient who has moved to that spot. Finally, the third night the character is moved into the exact same bed.

687. A good friend of an unnamed character has a life threatening disease that is set to take them before the year is up. Rather than spend the rest of their days suffering, the friend begs the character to kill them. When the character finally relents they immediately learn something about themselves – they quite enjoyed the act.

688. There have been many cases of serial killers that have hunted prostitutes for a number of different reasons, such as their hatred of the lifestyle. On the opposite end of the spectrum, there have also been cases in which prostitutes were actually serial killers themselves, such as Aileen Wuronos who preyed on truck drivers. Craft a narrative in which these two types of killers meet.

689. An investigation is launched when a crime scene uncovers hundreds of bodies, found in the deepest part of the woods. If that wasn't baffling enough similar crime scenes are also discovered all across the world.

690. Long before super max prisons, envision a scenario in which a massive hurricane destroys a wing of an old prison. Not only are petty criminals released but so is one of the worst murderers of all time.

691. A body is pulled out of a river after being spotted by a few fisherman. When the corpse undergoes an autopsy it is found to be filled with unusual objects: matches, chicken feet, stones, and more odds and ends. How did this come to be?

692. There are some houses that are to be avoided. Perhaps the lawns are too unkempt or the owner is too much of a recluse. Craft a narrative in which an unnamed character avoids this kind of house in lieu of asking the one next to it for directions. That, of course, is their mistake.

693. Many psychologists would be familiar with the name Kitty Genovese. This is a real murder case in which a woman was stabbed to death outside her apartment block, despite almost 40 people hearing the crime. When later questioned, each wrongfully assumed that someone else would render aide. Create a scenario in which a serial killer is well aware of the "bystander effect" and uses that to their advantage.

694. There arises a serial killer that is more terrifying than any that have come before. So much so that a group of criminals, even some murderers, work together to try and stop them.

695. "I delight in what I fear," is one of my favorite Shirley Jackson quotes. Suppose a serial killer holds that same mentality and goes after victims that remind them of their own fears and shortcomings.

696. Many are aware of the "writers are crazy" trope. Suppose this is indeed true for one such horror writer and they have hit a block in their work that can only be solved by acting out the crimes they write about.

697. There is some theories that state that one's personality will change after receiving an organ transplant, often taking on the characteristics of the deceased. Suppose this case with one unnamed character who cannot resist the urge to kill after receiving a criminal's heart.

698. While investigating a crime a detective discovers a fingerprint that doesn't match the victim and immediately believes this is the suspect. They log the print, find an address, but visiting the home turns up another victim – the same one bearing the strange fingerprint. This crime

scene also has another fingerprint that doesn't belong to either victims.

699. A serial killer is caught in the middle of their next murder by an unsuspecting off duty police officer. Although this could be the officer's big break if they bring the perp to justice, the serial killer also happens to be one of the wealthiest people on earth and makes them an offer that would end their financial troubles forever.

700. At the retirement home an elderly individual has been complaining about the other residents for some time. However, their complaints go on deaf ears. Soon the residents began to go missing and then one day they are found in pieces, hidden in a certain someone's closet.

701. Deciding to join a dating site an unnamed character meets someone incredibly charming and attractive, but there is just one fatal flaw – they also happen to be a serial killer. The irony is, the character is one too. Is this a match made in heaven...or hell?

702. A serial killer has been living in the shadows for quite some time and it is only recently that their victims have even been connected. As it turns out, the killer doesn't actually kill anyone, but convinces their victims to kill themselves.

703.   An aged serial killer knows that their time is coming to an end. They've managed to avoid capture for several decades and have killed roughly a few hundred people. However, they do not want to go gently into that good night and want to make this last slaying the biggest one yet.

704.   Serial killers are not known for their feelings of guilt, but after taking a new drug an unnamed character whose murdered hundreds is suddenly feeling remorse for everything they have ever done. The angst drives them crazier than they ever were and it is the researchers studying them that will have to bear the consequences.

705.   A serial killer has trapped their newest victim in what they deem their house of horrors. The only problem is that they've trapped a scary video game aficionado that seems to already have the floorplan mapped out.

706.   Medical advancements surpass what was thought possible when punishments were doled out. After serving 150 years in prison a notable serial killer is set free and doesn't look a day older than when they were incarcerated.

Cannibals

In many parts of the world cannibalism is still a viable cultural practice, whether it is the consumption of an enemy to prove one's power or of a loved one that has passed on to show respect. In addition, there have also been isolated incidences in which members of the human race has resorted to cannibalism in order to survive. That doesn't make it any less creepy though.

707. After winning a cruise vacation a couple eagerly accepts and takes off time for work. This is, as the note card reads, a once in a lifetime opportunity. On the first night on board the couple is told by fellow passengers that they simply must try the famous "hoomin" dish. Of course, they oblige. From then on, it's almost all they eat for dinner. It is until one of them accidentally chances into the kitchen that they realize what the strange meat to this dish is – people.

708. A young teen is sent by their parents to "fat camp." The parents hear that through hard work and targeted motivation, it would be a great way to lose weight and make some new friends. After some back and forth, the teen finally agrees. On their arrival they see a lot of very thin people walking around amongst the campers. These are the "champions", the ones who have managed to lose all the extra weight. That's the thing all other campers strive for. That is, until they learn that it isn't hard work and motivation that causes the weight loss, but by allowing it to be chopped off so the meat can be sold overseas.

709. In a similar scenario, suppose a character has been selling their own fat for years. They sell off chunks then rest and gain weight all over again just to make another few grand. Will this all catch up to the character, or is this a viable way to make a living?

710. On Halloween night, a young Trick or Treater stumbles across a man in a mask carving a pumpkin outside. Eagerly, the child races up, hoping to get a good haul, until they realize with horror that it isn't a pumpkin at all, but rather a human head.

711. There is a great deal of talk about the zombie apocalypse. So much so that there is a new disorder that emerges – one that causes one to not only think they are a zombie themselves, but they are strangely compelled to feast on the flesh of others.

712. After a heavy night of drinking and a tryst with a beautiful stranger, an unnamed character wakes up to find themselves tied to the bed. Their confusion is replaced with horror when their new lover comes in wearing an apron and holding a butcher knife.

713. A lonely unnamed character decides to pay a visit to a courtesan hoping that a night of wanton pleasure will do them some good. Things to go without a hitch except that

post-coitus the character begins to argue about the price. It's then that the courtesan reveals their true nature as a literal man-eater.

714. An unnamed character decides to hop a train in order to start life anew. They've picked a compartment at random and strangely this seems to be some type of ice compartment full of meat. Human meat.

715. "Soylent Green is people!" is a phrase that is most associate with literary cannibalism. It is especially harrowing because the population does not know they are being lied to about what they are eating. Put your own spin on this idea. How would the characters in your story be force fed some of their own kind and more importantly, how do they react?

716. An unnamed character has been placed in a POW camp after being found out by the enemy. Other prisoners are nothing but bone and it is clear that, once there, the prisoners are soon forgotten about. Very soon a fellow captive suggests they might eat the dead. If they don't, they too will die.

717. Use the above scenario, but change the situation slightly. Instead, it might be a starving town in the dead of winter or a hunting party trapped in a desolate location. What

then might happen if there is no longer any dying survivors and the dead must then turn to the living for sustenance?

718.   A group of friends are drinking at one of their houses late at night. Generally, this friend does not allow visitors but tonight they have made an exception after countless begging. When one of them gets up to go to the bathroom the owner quickly tells them to use the one in the bedroom and not the kitchen. Curiosity takes hold and they are unfortunate enough to discover human remains roasting in a pot.

719.   While playing in a ditch a group of kids come across a half-eaten corpse. Being children, they let curiosity take hold and inquisitively poke the body with a stick. The figure stirs in response and then very plainly coughs out a strained, "Help me."

720.   Children often grow up fearing the monster under the bed, the bogeyman, and the witch that lives in the gingerbread house. Create your own horror fairytale which utilizes the child-eater trope, but adds something new to this well-worn style of fable.

721.   In the middle of the apocalypse, an unnamed character stumbles across an old abandoned house. Thinking they

have found shelter they go to sleep in one of the many bedrooms, only to be later woken up by the sound of cannibals making a meal of a victim in the kitchen.

722. On a game show a contestant has finally made it to the very end. There is just one task that stands between them and the victory prize. The curtains are drawn back and the challenge is clear, they must eat the previous contestants.

723. An unnamed character is meeting their fiancée's family for the first time. Their apprehension is spot on, though not in the way they might have imagined it. As it turns out, their beloved comes from a family of cannibals.

724. An unnamed character is among an ancient tribe trying to migrate to an area that not only might be warmer, but may contain a better chance of hunting and foresting. Their efforts seem to be fruitless however and soon the group finds that they are slowly running out of food. There seems to be only one alternative.

725. While looking through the personals ad an unnamed character stumbles across an ad seeking someone to "eat." Thinking it to be some kind of joke the character responds, only to later find out that it isn't a joke at all.

726. With world resources dwindling a new law is set that human meat is not only legal, but it is highly encouraged. This is done through the consumption of the elderly and the infirmed. One group decides to fight back against the barbaric law.

727. In a similar scenario, suppose that the classic "A Modest Proposal" by Jonathan Swift is not a bit of satire, but is instead a viable solution to "the children of poor people from being a burthen to their parents or country, and for making them beneficial to the publick."

728. An unnamed character lives in a tribe where cannibalism is ritualistic in nature and occurs as a sign of respect for the dead. Someone close to them has just passed, but they are having deep reservations about taking their first bite.

729. An unnamed character is a teenager in a coming-of-age ceremony, expected to hunt, kill, and eat their given prey in front of the tribe. As it turns out, their prey ends up being their younger sibling.

730. While working in a traditional office setting an unnamed character notices that a co-worker always keeps one brown paper sack in the fridge with a note that says "MINE. KEEP AWAY." While this isn't uncommon in this environment, the character decides to take a peak,

curious about the lunch habits of their peer. They find a human hand.

731. A young unnamed character has been spending a lot of time living under a rock when it comes to sex. They have been extremely sheltered in this regard so are not familiar with certain idiomatic expressions. For instance, when they have sex for the first time they use the term "eating out" quite literally.

732. An unnamed character gets a job working at a morgue. They got the job to help with their own bills and although they were initially creeped out, the steady pay check is worth it. Turns out, they aren't scared at all when they see their first body on the table. They are hungry instead.

733. A small grocery chain has been struggling to compete against the largest box stores that are taking over the community. Vendor costs are too high and profits are too low. In order to save money one worker jokingly suggests stealing corpses and reselling it as cheap "extra organic meat". The plan is a hit.

734. In a similar vein, envision a case in which a small butcher shop has run into the same problem. However, their conclusion to use human meat occurs by happenstance.

While grinding down a large volume of meat a worker has a little accident, and the rest as they say, is history.

735. In order to curb the growing homeless population, a controversial city ordinance emerges. One is able to kill any homeless individual on site so long as the food is reused for sustenance.

736. An unnamed character has become quite obsessed with the very notion of cannibalism and finally decide they must try human flesh. This of course requires them to locate and dispatch of a victim. Which they botch horribly.

737. Similarly, suppose an unnamed character does not want to kill anyone, but still wants to know what human meat might taste like. In order to reach a compromise with that need and their own mortality they decide to try the closest human available – themselves.

738. There are many different tribes that eat humans for some type of cultural purpose; be it for power, respect, or something else entirely. Craft a narrative from the point of view of an outsider witnessing these acts for the very first time.

739. While working at a hospital during a late night shift an attendant is making their rounds when they hear the sound of moaning coming from one of the rooms. Thinking a patient might be in trouble they rush in the room and their suspicions to prove to be correct. The patient isn't just injured, they are actively eating themselves.

740. A group of schoolchildren are visiting a living history type of town when one of them decides to sneak off from the group. They stumble across the stuff of nightmares; a group of cannibals eating their dinner.

741. An adrenaline junky decides to investigate rumours of a cannibal cult deep in one of the more desolate parts of town. After a few hours of not finding anything they finally spot the group, already in mid-feast. Instantly their heart goes from 0 to 60, but not just because these people actually exist. Rather because the characters knows them.

742. An unnamed character goes on an expedition deep in the jungle in hopes to find signs of a lost civilization. Just when they hear something rustling in the bushes they are knocked over the head and they wake up they find themselves in a cage, a boiling pot of water simmering in anticipation.

Home Invasion

The call is coming from inside the house! Home invasion is a popular trope that shows up in a lot of horror cinema, but it's also appears in horror fiction as well. This goes back to the idea of control and how, as humans, we are desperate to keep it. When it involves our home, the very thing that is supposed to offer the most security, it can be downright terrifying when that control is lost.

743.   A unnamed character rents low income housing after finally deciding to take the plunge and move out from their parents' home. It's easy enough to ignore the bugs, perpetually dripping faucet, and mold growing in weird places, but what really bothers them is the knock on the door at exactly 2 am every night. After weeks of this torment they finally decide to buckle down one night and call their parents the next time they hear another nightly knock. This time it isn't a knock at the door they hear, but the turning of a knob.

744.   An unnamed character wakes up in an enclosed, hot space. Thankfully, they happen to have a lighter in their pocket, which allows them to investigate their surroundings. They're in a coffin. Buried deep in their own backyard.

745. After a stressful day, an unnamed character has decided to spend the rest of it relaxing. They pull up their favorite horror movie and set the volume as loud as it will go. They don't seem to notice that there is a face in the window that mirrors the face onscreen.

746. After a robbery at their home occurs, an unnamed character decides to spend the night at their significant other's house. Unfortunately, the culprit doesn't care about the items in the home and soon follows the character to their SO's house too.

747. During a party one of the guests runs into the living room screaming. The others follow them to the kitchen where muffled cries are coming from outside. Inside, embedded on the window's glass, is a flailing arm. One of the guests grabs an axe, intending to teach the would-be burglar a lesson.

748. It's the night before Christmas and all through the house not a creature is stirring except for the cat burglar dressed in a Santa suit. They've done this to a few houses now, but this time an unwitting homeowner turns the fireplace on at exactly the wrong minute.

749. A home invasion goes horribly wrong when a cat burglar breaks into what they think is an unoccupied home. The

owner is indeed there, hanging from the rafters after committing suicide.

750. For weeks a window is broken and alarms go off while an unnamed character is at work. Thankfully, nothing is stolen, but it's getting annoying having to constantly replace the glass. The character decides to wait home to catch the culprit in the act. Turns out, that's exactly what they want.

751. "Please, I'll give you anything you want," The homeowner cries. The criminal demands answers. Answers they will never get because the crook has the wrong house.

752. An elderly character has moved six times in their life and each time they have been robbed. Is this a case of really, really bad luck or does someone just have it out for them?

753. Envision a scenario where a city is deemed the safest on Earth because no crime has ever happened there. Suppose all of that changes one terrible night when several houses are attacked at once.

754. A couple is brutally attacked in their home by a crazed madman. Thankfully, neither of them are hurt and their possessions are all safe and sound. Then the couple discovers that their baby is missing.

755.   "You're a monster," an unnamed character screams at their attacker. The attacker grins widely, seeing it as a challenge. Just how far will they go to show the victim what a monster really is?

756.   A group of unnamed characters finds themselves in their own basement, hands tied firmly behind their backs. The attackers clean out the entire house and then grab one character claiming this will be their hostage. Truth is, that character is actually in cahoots with the culprits.

757.   A teenager has headphones on with the music's volume on full blast. They don't hear their family calling for help, nor do they hear the sound of footsteps as a stranger enters their bedroom door. It isn't until the stranger reaches out and turns off the music that they notice anything at all.

758.   During a home invasion, an unnamed character takes matters in their own hands and defends themselves against their attackers, killing one. The other burglars run off, leaving the character face-to-face with their guilt.

759.   An unnamed character is working from home when there's several loud knocks at the door. Thinking it might be the plumber, the reason why they took the day off in the first place, they swing open the door. Several large

figures with guns then barrel past them. Behind them is a very badly injured plumber.

760.   An unnamed character comes home from work to find their entire family bound and gagged. They immediately pull out their phone, but they have no signal. The criminal is somewhere in the house, watching them, but where?

761.   Round after round of ammunition has been emptied into a home invader. The home owner has prepared for this moment the day they bought their new weapon. There's just one problem – the home invader isn't a criminal at all, but rather a very surprised houseguest.

762.   A young unnamed character wakes up their parents in the dead of night. "There's a stranger!" Their parents assume it's just a bad dream. It isn't a bad dream, though. Now that very stranger has made their way inside the bedroom where the child nestles in between their parents, who desperately want to get back to sleep.

763.   An unnamed character makes their living robbing houses. It isn't the most noble of occupations, but it pays the bills. Then one night, *their* house gets broken into. Is this a case of karmic justice or one of revenge?

764. As part of their nightly regime, an unnamed character covers their face with a charcoal mask, complete with cucumbers over their eyes. Unbeknownst to the character, someone has been watching them the whole time and is waiting for this beauty ritual to be finished before they make their move.

765. One of the scariest fears, when it comes to home invasion, is to look out the window randomly and see a face looking back. Let's up the stakes a bit, shall we? Envision a scenario in which a character doesn't just see one face, but they see a face in each and every window of their home.

766. In order to escape a murderer who's broken into their home, an unnamed character runs to a neighbor's house. The neighbor is more than happy to let them in, but once the character is inside the neighbor becomes increasingly agitated and won't let them use to the phone to call the police. It seems the character has escaped one horrible situation by moving on to the next.

767. A group of children are home alone when a gang of crooks break in. The children must be resourceful against these criminals or they will all perish.

768. An unnamed character is completely immobilized by the ropes that bind their hands and feet. If that wasn't bad

enough, before the criminals left they set the house on fire.

769.   When a teenager sneaks out of the house at night they only expected a good time at their friend's party. However, they unwittingly avoid a masked stranger entering the home just as they leave it. When they come back they find out their family has been massacred.

770.   It's the Old South and a lynch mob is trying to pull out an unnamed character from their home. Suppose this mob has been expected and soon they will pay severely for their hatred.

771.   A break-in happens at a sorority house while the members are sleeping. One wakes up and finds a masked stranger standing over their bed. They immediately think it's a prank. A mistake that might cost all of them their lives.

772.   Two families have been feuding with each other over something that happened generations ago. Then one night one family decide to rob the other's house. It just so happens that the other family is doing the exact same thing.

773. The sound of glass breaking rouses an unnamed character from their sleep. They reach for their trusty gun only to find it's already missing.

774. An unnamed character steps out of the shower to find their home has been broken into in that short time span. What's worse is that they find several pictures of themselves taken by the culprit, and one especially creepy selfie of the intruder.

775. For several days an unnamed character feels like something is amiss. Items are constantly moved or missing. The worst part is that they live alone so there is no one else to blame. Finally, they realize they aren't as alone as they thought they were when video from a surveillance camera they set up proves otherwise.

776. After cleaning their child's room, a parent discovers a hidden camera. Panicked they call the police. Whoever committed the heinous act had to be close to them.

777. An unnamed character wakes up tied to a chair after being knocked unconscious upon arriving home. Before them an intruder taunts and tortures them. The intruder's voice sounds so very *familiar*.

778. An unnamed character cups their hands over their mouth
to keep from crying out as they see an intruder's footsteps
near the bed they are hiding under. After what seem like
eons they hear a door slam. They make a run for it, not
realizing that there is more than one intruder and only
one has left.

Strange Crime

Although most horror fiction deals with murderous crime,
other types of crime can be equally scary. Theft, arson, stalking,
assault, and all manners of criminal mischief can be emotionally
taxing on the victim, even years after the event has occurred. Just
about any crime can be used in horror; the key is to find the part
of it that leaves a general feeling of dread and then weave that
into the narrative.

779. An unnamed teen is mortified to learn that they will be
moving and their senior year is going to be spent at a
brand new high school. The first day, however, isn't so
bad. They make new friends and find out their classes are
all very fun and exciting. It is just near lunchtime that
they notice a kid staring at them strangely. Passing it off
as nothing they decide to go about their business. While
waiting for the bus they see the kid again, this time
standing behind a tree. When they go home they tell their
parents who then alert the principal. When the character
goes back the next day, they are assured there's nothing to

worry about – there's no student here that fits that description.

780. When depositing money at the bank an unnamed character finds themselves in the middle of a bank robbery. In order to make their getaway one of the robbers grabs the character and makes a break for it, with their brand new hostage.

781. An unnamed character is travelling in a new town. To keep their travel expenses low they steal from a local shop only to be quickly found out. Their only 'trial' is an angry mob seeking vengeance. What's worse is the punishment itself which quickly becomes a litany of screaming.

782. During an infamous "Mischief Night" a group of teenagers are out playing pranks – throwing eggs, setting car alarms, and leaving toilet paper trails hanging from the trees wherever they go. Soon however their crimes go from mildly annoying to downright evil.

783. A group of unnamed characters join a suicide pact; each with their own reasons. However, during the actual event one character decides not to go through with it. Before long they find themselves surrounded by a cluster of bodies and a story no one seems to believe.

784.	In a similar scenario, suppose a character decides to take their own life and succeeds – somewhat. They are dead only for a brief time, but since they went through with the act they are charged for the crime.

785.	While at a remote gas station an unnamed character is accosted by a stranger demanding money. What this criminal doesn't realize is that the character has already committed a robbery of their own.

786.	An unnamed character is called to jury duty and having no viable excuses, they reluctantly go. Halfway in the trial their interest is suddenly piqued when they realize the accused is on trial for crimes they themselves have committed.

787.	After one of the crown jewels of the campus receives only six months for a sexual assault a group of students decide to take the law into their own hands. Soon the student awakens in a dark room, tied to a chair.

788.	An unnamed character decides to take a walk after a restless night. They stumble across a neighbor dragging large trash bags into their house. They think nothing of it until a few nights later they hear on the news that several bodies are missing from the local cemetery.

789. While driving on the freeway an unnamed character sees the trunk of the car in front of them bumping unnaturally.

790. While out on a date an unnamed character notices that their potential mate acts more and more apprehensive as the night wears on. It isn't until several hours in that it's discovered that the date has been stealing from each place the two have gone to.

791. One morning an unnamed character comes home to find their home broken into, but nothing stolen. The first time the character's furniture is completely rearranged, and the next there are new clothes in the character's closet. On the third night two strange children are sitting at the dinner table and someone is cooking dinner. Looking at the character they proudly exclaim, "Hi honey. Welcome home!"

792. An unnamed character has a horrible kleptomania habit and will steal even the most trivial items. One day they find themselves stealing from the wrong people. The crimes committed will cost them their hands.

793. A small child born to the streets survives by becoming a pick pocket. One day they pick the pocket of the wrong person and soon find themselves in the trunk of a car.

794. In a similar scenario, craft a narrative in which a child from the streets routinely stores their collection in a makeshift shelter. One night they find that their collection of miscellaneous junk has become a sentient monster.

795. A stalker has been finding different victims to emotionally torture for quite some time. However, one day they notice someone dressed in black outside their window and in a flash they're gone. The same thing happens at work, while going to the grocery store, and so forth. It seems the stalker has become the stalkee.

796. Tiredly, an unnamed character goes into the grocery store to get a few things. After checking out they make it halfway to their car before they are surrounded by the manager and two security guards. They are told pointedly that they will now be arrested for stealing from the store, even though they have just paid for all of the items. No matter what they say, their fate remains clear.

797. A cop questions his own mental sanity when he continues to arrest the same burglar over and over again. Though each time the criminal doesn't seem to recognize the cop. This goes on for months.

798.   After a particularly elusive white tail is caught a group of
        hunters go out to a local bar to celebrate only to come
        across an individual abusing an animal outside of it.
        Although the hunters try to get the person to stop,
        because of the irony of the situation, they refuse.

799.   When a fire breaks out in the neighborhood most chalk it
        up to bad luck. However, one by one homes nearby go up
        in flames every couple of nights. Clearly there is an arson
        at large, but no one has any idea who it could be.

800.   An unnamed character hires a mechanic and then pays
        with a bad check. Whether or not they actually knew it
        was a bad check is a moot point as soon they find the
        brakes in their car has been cut.

801.   An unnamed character has the strange habit of stealing
        underwear from their neighbors. One night they sneak in
        the house to steal a fresh pair when they come across
        several dead bodies. The crime in this scenario can
        certainly change, such as it being a robber, rapist, etc.

802.   A pick pocket steals a wallet from a random stranger, but
        instead of money they find a note that reads, "Didn't your
        mother ever tell you not to take things that don't belong
        to you?" The thief shrugs it off and picks another pocket,
        this time swiping a coin purse. Opening it they find

another note which reads, "I warned you. Now I'm going to take something from you." Unsettled, but determined they yank a purse this time. A note falls from it. It reads, "Your life."

803. An unnamed character finds themselves abducted from a parking lot and placed in a locked room. Surprisingly, the character has been kidnapped by themselves. How is this possible?

804. Two small time crooks set up a perfect get rich scheme. Everything should go well, and the two could make a great deal of money. That is until one of them screws up. Then things turn deadly.

805. After illegally poaching a rare species a hunter is knocked unconscious and when they wake they find themselves in the middle of the woods. When they hear the click of a gun they realize with horror that is their turn to be hunted.

806. After a drunken night of revelry an unnamed character gets into a car crash, killing an entire family. They are consumed by grief, but if this wasn't bad enough one of the members has not only survived, but wants revenge.

807. After two young characters steal candy from what seems like a small, unsupervised convenience store, the lights go out. The try to leave but the doors are locked. Fearfully, they turn around to see a pair of glowing yellow eyes staring in the dark, behind the counter.

808. An unnamed character sells a new drug to a small group of teens at a party. The group shares the drug and soon almost everyone has ingested the substance. Just when the dealer is about to leave they hear screaming and just like that many of the kids have dropped to the ground, convulsing and spitting in agony.

809. Hoping to make some fast cash on the black market, a museum intern steal an ancient Mayan artefact from the newest exhibition. They are beyond mortified when they come home to find a snarling leopard in the living room of their apartment.

810. A college punk decides to impersonate a police officer for the fun of it. Soon, however they get an unsettling surprise when they find themselves the target of a deranged cop killer with a strange agenda.

811. An abuser comes home to find that their children have gone missing and in their place is a pack of wild and feral

dogs. At the sound of the screams from somewhere outside giggling can be heard.

812. A teen charged with truancy is sent to a strange school where student who don't reform, die.

813. An unnamed character sees flashing lights in their rear-view mirror and instantly pulls to the side of the road. After checking their license the officer makes an arrest. It's clearly a case of mistaken identity, but no one seems to believe the character.

814. Envision a scenario in which a character wakes from a coma without realizing that the laws have completely changed while they were under. No matter what they do, they can't seem to stop committing unlawful acts and eventually it catches up to them.

Visceral

This type of horror is often known by the term "splatterpunk." In the film genre, there are many "exploitation films" that also fit this theme. Quite simply, these storylines are very thin and the focus is instead on the horrible, gory, sickening, and essentially, anything that disgusts or shocks the audience. Typically, horror is supposed to come with some sense of dread, but these are notable because they serve no other purpose. When crafting these tales it's important to remember that an audience goes into splatter fiction knowing that gore takes front and center, so one can be a little more liberal with what horrible plot devices are used.

815. "And here we are folks, a real live murder about to take place." It's the only words spoken before the unnamed character adjusts the camera and pans to the table where a helpless victim is tied by all four limbs. There's no pause, no breath, simply no transition between the simple statement and the sound of hacking to be heard.

816. One of the most common Halloween games asks players to feel various objects while blindfolded in order to guess what they might be. Of course, the objects are supposed to be completely different, and more spooky, than what they actually are. For instance, peeled grapes are no longer grapes, but eyeballs. Envision a scenario where this game is played, but the objects are very real.

817. There have been cases in which an individual does not receive the correct anesthesia dosage and thus, they wake up during surgery. In a similar scenario, suppose this happens to an unnamed character – but during their own autopsy.

818. Splatterpunk has often been said to be a result of our times. That the modern generations are simply more prone to glorifying horror because it is everywhere. Using

this type of logic, set your story in a violence-limited society. Perhaps even some type of Utopia. Make the violence that does occur that much more horrifying as a result.

819. An unnamed character comes home to find blood and gore everywhere. On the walls, the furniture, and even on the ceiling. The strangest part is that they live alone.

820. After several calls from an unlisted number an unnamed character finally picks up the phone. All they can hear on the other end is the sounds of their loved ones screaming before a click occurs.

821. After years of trying, an undercover journalist finally manages to attend a "burn show." Up until this point, they've only been met with speculation on what it might be. Nothing prepares them for seeing victims being led into glass cages, surrounded by rows upon rows of rich spectators, and then being burned alive for entertainment purposes.

822. In horror writing, there is the school of thought that nothing is as scary as the reader's own imagination. Craft a scenario in which an unnamed character is placed in total darkness. Rely on sensory details that do not involve sight in order to describe the torture that will take place.

823. Desperate to lose weight, an unnamed character joins a health club that is supposed to "slice the fat right off." Little do they know, the ad means literally.

824. An extremely talented artist is known around the world for their interesting spin on traditional splatter painting. One night a young apprentice walks in on the artist in the midst of creating such a work. That's when they discover the paint used in the art comes from the fluids of still warming bodies.

825. Envision a scenario in which humanity is so over-populated that many families live in high-rise buildings that often reach 20 floors easily. Each has formed their own little community. One such building has decided to curb the population to allow new entrants. A lottery is drawn every year and the unlucky floor picked will face a complete massacre to make room for the next generation.

826. Suppose that overpopulation isn't as big a problem as limited resources. In order to help with the need for fuel corpses are now used, but only one unwitting character stumbles onto this fact. By finding bodies being loaded into a giant vat.

827. An unnamed character has just gotten a new job as a morgue attendant. Everything seems fine until they discover the current morgue supervisor has been using the corpses to fulfil their own carnal pleasures.

828. After a year's investigation a journalist finally gets enough information on a prison to prove the institution has been torturing the inmates there. Before they can go to the press, or even the authorities, they are abducted themselves. Now they will get a first-hand account of how terrifying the situation really is.

829. After their fingers have been removed, their legs broken, and a series of deep cuts litter their bodies, a torture victim finally succumbs to death. It's no matter because in this scenario they are simply reanimated so the process can start all over again.

830. A young actor(ess) down on their luck signs up for a new film. A snuff film. They are told that it will be mostly "harmless", but soon they will discover how false that statement actually is.

831. Perhaps no story crafted can be as horrifying as real life. I once had a creative writing professor that only used the most macabre news headlines to craft her short stories.

Do the same. Take one of the most disturbing articles you can find and then process it through your work.

832. In war, there is the idea that anything goes, whether right or wrong. Take the perspective from a captain sent to interrogate a prisoner of war by any means necessary.

833. An unnamed character is excitedly roaming around downtown in a new city. That is until several large objects begin hitting the asphalt all around them. It's bodies. Hundreds of them.

834. An art collector walks down the length of a personal gallery, headed towards their newest arrival. At the end of the corridor is a fresh corpse entombed in glass. The collector sighs appreciatingly and stars into the lifeless face on the other side. To them, watching the bodies decay is the most organic form of art on Earth.

835. Back in the days of the electric chair, a violent criminal is put to death. Well, kind of. Each time the lever is pulled, they are burned severely but can't seem to die. How long will this torture last before they are finally put out of their misery?

836. While exploring a dark cave an unknown character discovers a puzzle box that will give them their heart's

desire. So long as they are willing to make one blood sacrifice each time.

837. An individual attempts suicide using a shot-gun. Seconds after the gun goes off they regret their decision and desperately want to live. Somehow the universe gives into their inner pleas, but they are now missing their lower jaw.

838. After a head injury, an unnamed character has an insatiable need to revel in the 7 deadly sins. This, of course, comes at a cost because they can't seem to control these innate desires.

839. For years a young character has been chained up in the basement of a sick individual. One day they manage to escape only to return years later to get revenge in the most horrific way possible.

840. Craft a scenario that takes the point of view of a vicious murderer. After massacring an entire family they realize a member has escaped. They set out on a course to track down and kill this one witness.

841. There were many horrific torture methods employed throughout history. Use one of these and showcase the perspective of a victim, desperate to survive with, at the

very least, their life. For example, a character has been tied to a tree while a pack of hungry dogs are released nearby.

842. An unnamed character wakes up in a cold sweat dreaming that a loved one is being tortured downstairs. They think it's nothing more than a disturbing nightmare until they hear the sound of screaming.

843. A homeless character is searching through the town dump when they come across a corpse. Rather than call the police they decide that the body would make good company instead. They are so *very* lonely.

844. With only a few days left to live terminal character does something they've always dreamed of doing – go on a mass killing spree.

845. Perhaps you've heard of H.H. Holms, the serial killer that used a hotel of his own design to torture and kill his victims. Suppose a hotel actually exists and an unnamed character must escape each disturbing room to get out.

846. A grave keeper is arrested, but not for what you might think. Yes, they do indeed take it upon themselves to use the corpses, but only to make intricate pieces of art. Sometimes they fuse together the corpses with other

animals that have been put under the care of a taxidermist.

847.   While on an expedition, an explorer finds something horrifying – a trapped individual who has barely managed to survive inside a deep hole for years.

848.   Craft a scenario from the perspective of death. Yes, *that* Death. Imagine what extreme acts of brutality they must have seen throughout the existence of humankind.

Werewolves, & Other Supernatural Beings.

The inclusion of supernatural beings primarily factors into the classic famous monsters, such as Dracula or Frankenstein or the gothic horror that tends to blend darkness and romance. This is largely where paranormal romance comes from. However, this is not quite horror because the emphasis is on relationship building, no matter how strange, rather than on the beings as a horror device. When used in horror, supernatural beings don't necessarily have to be frightening themselves, but they should still create a sense of fear for the audience. This can be because of their appearance, their actions, or what happens as a result of their presence. In addition, it's important to bring something new to the table when dealing with these supernatural beings, especially those that often spring up in horror.

Witches

Although they are often associated with religious connotations, witches and witchcraft does not necessarily involve any kind of religiosity. In this case, any human that is endued with magical powers can be considered a witch, and sometimes in the case of males, a warlock. Though "witch" is generally a gender neutral term itself. When using this supernatural being in these narrative prompts, the focus is on the powers, whether or not there is any kind of an association with the occult.

849. While escaping from a group of bullies a teen enters a shop that, from the outside, looks like a boring bookstore. On the inside, however, there is no book in sight and instead, there is a collection of strange flasks, bottles, cauldrons and a wide range of various plants and small ingredients in jars. If the teen is looking for help, they are a little out of luck because the stranger behind the counter instantly goes into a tirade, screaming about the mortal that has entered the sacred realm.

850. A new witch has just begun harnessing their powers and tries out a new spell which immediately backfires. Thankfully, they don't die, but they come pretty close.

851. It's a witches' gathering, where all manners of beings come together to worship Satan. Each must bring a sacrifice and the witch with the weakest offering will take the place of their own poor gift.

852. A witch has put a curse on an unnamed character. Each day the character finds a new boil in a different spot. It

isn't until they are covered head to foot do they find out who's behind the madness.

853. In the dead of night, a young parent goes to check on their newborn, quietly asleep in the nursery. They are too late – an old crone is already sneaking the babe away.

854. Nature is beautiful. At least it's supposed to be. While in the woods a hiker comes across a collection of dead frogs, then two dead foxes, a dead deer, and finally the witch responsible for it all.

855. A witch attempts to curse a foe over and over again, assuming their spell must not be working correctly. What they don't realize is that it's definitely working, but it will take time before the spells manifest in the victim. All at once.

856. An unnamed character finds a strange wart that appears on their skin randomly. They assume it's a problem that will go away on its own until one night they wake up to find a creature suckling on it.

857. A busybody has a nasty habit of spying on their neighbors. When an elderly character moves in they are somewhat disappointed because there won't be any juicy gossip.

That changes when they peek out their window to see the character bathing nude in the light of the full moon.

858.   A group of miscreants jump out of a truck and begin to attack a young character walking home from school. Luckily the character is a very powerful witch who's just about to have a brand new skill manifest.

859.   Many witches choose to commune with nature as a part of their practice. While many witches accept that mankind often destroys it, one witch is simply not satisfied with this quiet acceptance and makes it a point to destroy all who dare come against Mother Nature.

860.   Witches are often depicted as being traditionally ugly with warts, hooked shaped noses, and greasy hair. Suppose that's true and in revolt traditionally beautiful people suddenly start disappearing the world over.

861.   A black cat is seen every day in front of an unnamed character's window. They don't seem to notice the animal nor do they realize that they have committed a slight against the witch the familiar belongs to.

862.   At a hardware store an unnamed character asks to see the doors available for purchase. They are helped but it becomes increasingly clear something is off. Finally the

witch reveals that the door is for a spell. One that will soon bring forth an ancient monster through it.

863. "Eat it, just take one more bite. Come on, love. You can do it." The words sound nice enough. Told to the elderly patient inside a nursing home. It's too bad they are spoken by a witch who is using these poor souls as test subjects for their latest potions.

864. Envision a scenario in which a coming of age witch is allowed to choose their own familiar. While normally witches want toads, black cats, or crows, this witch is about to pick an extremely dangerous and deadly predator.

865. A witch allows passer-by's to use their garden for nourishment, never letting on to the fact that half of it is poisonous. It's a gamble as to whether or not the garden will kill these visitors.

866. An unnamed character sneaks into a witch's cottage in order to escape the heavy rain. Over the open flame in the fireplace they find a cooking pot with a delicious smelling stew inside. They are so hungry they decide a quick bite won't hurt and open the top, only to scream and drop it immediately. Inside are the pieces of missing neighborhood children.

867.	A witch begins to lose control of their powers. It starts with a sneeze that lights the curtains on fire and ends with three people dead.

868.	A plague of witches fly across the city on their broomsticks, cackling all the while. They are harvesting villagers, but for what?

869.	A witch begins to dream walk, visiting the sleep images of others at will. It's a surreal yet beautiful experience until the witch waltzes into a nightmare for the first time. That's when they realize their physical body can be harmed, even killed.

870.	While cleaning out their grandparent's attic a dusty old book is discovered. It's not just any book, but a grimoire. Complete with all kinds of spells from charms to outright death curses.

871.	A powerful witch has been entombed for thousands of years. After finally getting free they immediately seek revenge on the descendants of those that put them away.

872.	A witch's apprentice is tasked with finding all the ingredients needed for a spell. The witch carefully instructs them to only get one item at a time without looking ahead. The apprentice can't help themselves and reads the last line on the list, "Your still beating heart."

873.   Envision a world in which witches have special talents that separate them from each other. One is good at curses, one at potions, and unnamed character seems to especially good at sacrificing humans.

874.   A witch decides that they want to give up the practice altogether. In order to do so they must convert someone else to take their place. Even if the chosen person is unwilling.

875.   A young unnamed character sneaks outside to go explore the woods outside their home. They come across a clearing were a coven a witches is sacrificing a screaming victim. The character instantly tries to make a hasty retreat, but steps on a branch, causing all of the witches in the vicinity to snap their heads over.

876.   An unnamed character visits a local witch to help them with a little problem. The witch suggests a reading of their future, to which the character promptly agrees to. Out comes the runes, but amongst them is a human finger.

877. A witch is blessed with the second sight. They are able to see an omen over the door of one set to die. One day they suddenly see this omen on every door.

878. While out flying on their broomstick an unnamed character spots a poor soul being abused. They decide to take matters into their own hands and murders the individuals responsible in the most horrific way possible.

879. An unnamed character has a number of pets in their home, from cats to pigs. It's eventually found out that this character is not only a witch but all of their "pets" are cursed humans.

880. A witch is suddenly ripped from their home and dragged kicking and screaming to the stake by a group of angry and hateful villagers. This is all an act of course. The witch has been dancing in fire for years.

881. A pregnant witch is rushed to the hospital when their water breaks. When the baby is pulled out, everyone in the room screams. It's a pig. Alternatively, this scenario works for any nonhuman (or creepily, more than human) newborn.

882. A witch goes to the doctor complaining of a toothache. The doctor insists that they should stop eating so much

sugar. The witch, of course, blames this generation's penchant for giving children so much candy.

883. A lone witch has been keeping terrifying creatures at bay, in their own realm. All that changes when the witch dies.

884. Two witches are in a fierce battle, which continues to escalate. It wouldn't be as bad if half the city's population didn't die as a result.

885. An old crone appears on the doorstep of an unnamed character quite randomly. Before the character can get a word in, the witch mutters, "It's yours now" and then dies. Pushed in the character's hand is a grimoire.

886. A 100 year old witch figures out a spell to make herself young again. However, they seem to have trouble adjusting to their new 19 year old body.

887. The high priestess of a witches' coven is nearing the end of the ritual when they begin to have second thoughts. The knife in their hands begin to shake and the infant wails louder.

Werewolves & Shapeshifters

A lycanthrope, or werewolf is a human that can transform into a wolf or wolf-like creature through a curse or some other artificial means. In general, werewolves are the most common type of shapeshifters, though there are others across many different cultures. For instance, in many folktales a human is transformed into an animal, such as a frog or serpent, through some kind of curse. In other cultures, a shapeshifter is a shaman type of individual who can change at will into the animal of their choosing. Every once in a while, a shapeshifter is also notable because they do not transform into an animal at all, but rather something else entirely.

888.   During one misty morning an unnamed character decides to head to the local dog park despite the heavy fog. Once there, their small dog begins to back up, whining loudly and refusing to go into their favorite spot. As some of the mist clears the character understands why – a large burling wolf, with a human-like face, is busy making a meal out of its most recent victim.

889.   An unnamed character is given an extremely large dog to care for. It isn't a dog though. It's a werewolf in the witness protection program.

890.   Craft a scenario in which an unnamed character has just been turned into a werewolf and has trouble controlling their bloodlust every full moon.

891.   An athlete is determined to bulk up for next season. They've tried everything, but it still doesn't seem to be

enough. Out of desperation, they visit a shady clinic that will give them a blood transfusion. Using a wolf.

892. Every month an unnamed character's spouse goes on a business trip. After several months the character demands answers, assuming they are cheating. That's when the spouse admits that they are faithful, but also a werewolf.

893. An unnamed character wakes up to find their spouse's side of the bed empty. They hear the sound of cracking and immediately go to investigate. The noise is that of bones breaking, made possible by their werewolf spouse eating another family member.

894. A vegan wakes up in the middle of the forest. Next to them lies the corpse of a ravaged deer.

895. An unnamed character has been summoned by their pack. Normally this wouldn't be cause for concern, but then they arrive the character is told they will be leading the attack on much stronger pack.

896. "No, no, no," An unknown character screams, holding their slain beloved. They know they are responsible, but have no idea that they are a werewolf.

897.   During a routine check-up a doctor is astonished to find a previously sickly character now the embodiment of perfect health. Except for the bitemarks of course.

898.   An unnamed character has tried medication, holistic therapies, and even witchcraft, but his is all to no avail. Every full moon it happens again.

899.   A zoo is in for a surprise when a naked character suddenly appears in the newest exhibit. Amidst all the commotion nobody seems to notice there is a wolf missing.

900.   An unnamed character makes a mad dash down the street before turning into a dark alley. There they hit a dead end. Behind them the snarls and growls are getting closer.

901.   There is a great deal of dispute regarding how a werewolf physically changes from a person to a creature. Do the bones break and then reform? Is it purely magic? No matter, a scientist believes they have found the answer and are now using normal humans as test subjects to prove their theory correct.

902.   After a loved one's burial a family is tasked with cleaning out their estate. Curiously they find a locked room that has broken furniture, chains, and claw marks everywhere.

903. When a werewolf turns from a creature to an animal, it's supposed to be an extremely painful process. Investigate this. Craft a narrative that focuses on the pain itself and what kind of psychological trauma that might cause as a result.

904. There is no doubt that many werewolf narratives are extremely narrow because they are based off similar legends. Research werewolves of different cultures and break the norm.

905. An unnamed character begins to howl in the middle of a classroom before transforming. Not only is it the middle of the day, but it's not even a full moon. What's going on?

906. An unnamed character has a problem with their new condition. It isn't the bloodlust so much as it is the little things. The need to chase after anything that's thrown, chewing with their mouth open and smacking, wagging their bottom when they get too excited, and howling while laughing.

907. A pregnant character bursts into tears while being examined by their doctor. In response, the doctor asks what's wrong, assuming it might be the baby. The character admits that they are a werewolf and are worried that the baby might be one too.

908. Suppose werewolves are now so common that 1 out of 5 people are one. As a result, werewolves are the dominate species and humans are nothing more than walking burgers, kept for convenient food.

909. Suppose there are many different types of werecreatures. For example, an unnamed character is a weremouse and must fight for survival every full moon.

910. An unnamed character soon finds themselves in the hospital after a wolf attack. They will indeed become a werewolf. That is, if they don't succumb to their injuries first.

911. An astronaught is sent to the moon before realizing they are a werewolf. Once there they become a super charged wolf. More powerful than anything the world has seen before.

912. Several werewolves are kept as prisoners, forced to fight each other in a cage match. An unnamed character finds themselves there for the first time.

913. Using the above scenario, suppose the werewolves manage to get free and are going to get revenge on everyone inside the arena, including the audience.

914. A werewolf imprints on the one they wish to be their mate. Problem is, their intended wants nothing to do with them.

915. An unnamed character takes a trip to the zoo. The animals there seem agitated whenever the character is nearby. Although they aren't sure why then, they might just figure out the next full moon.

916. An unnamed character has just gotten married, not realizing that they've just been initiated into a family of shapeshifters.

917. A shapeshifter can turn into any animal it chooses. One day they make the mistake of turning into an insect and are caught by a small child.

918. An unnamed character is visited by a different animal from the woods almost every day. However, when they become severely injured in a freak accident the shapeshifter must break form to take them to the hospital.

919. A shapeshifter has been using their ability to sneak into houses in order to rob them. One night they inadvertently end up into the home of another, much more powerful, shapeshifter.

920.   A shapeshifer has figured out how to shift into animals that don't even exist. Suppose they choose to turn into a dragon, but as a result they are compelled to burn those around them.

921.   An unnamed character sees a strange silhouette in the window every night. They can easily pass it off as nothing because it's a different animal each time. They assume it's just their tired imagination, but it isn't. It's a shapeshifter.

922.   Each day, the mail carrier must deal with a barking, aggressive dog. Then one day the dog is no longer there, but in its place lies a naked and dead human.

923.   An unnamed character has a chance to interview a shapeshifter. The interview is going well, until the interviewee changes without warning and seems very, very hungry.

924.   While being intimate together an unnamed character is shocked when their partner suddenly turns into an animal.

925.   Desperate to become a shapeshifter, an unnamed character seeks out a small pack of them. The group

promises to turn the character, but this just a trap. Really they are always on the lookout for desperate fresh meat.

926.   An unnamed character finds a dead animal on their doorstep each day. What's more curious is that these animals range in sizes. First there is a squirrel, then a rabbit, a fox, even a deer. Turns out, it's a secret admirer who happens to also be a werewolf.

Vampires

Lately, vampires seem to be thrust into the paranormal romance genre and can't seem to shake free. This is a shame really, because the original vampire tales were downright horrifying. Bloated corpses and pallor stricken individuals that creep through the night and don't always bite their victims with a tender, loving nip. It's messy. Real messy. When you weave through this section, try not to think of these creatures as misunderstood bad guys, but rather focus on them for what they truly are – demon-like entities that are so detached from humanity that they have become predators themselves.

927.   The young child screams in the dead of night so that their parents come running into the room. "There's a monster at the window!" The child claims. Their parents, tired and worn from the day, promise that it's nothing and tuck the youngster back into bed. Only it *is* something, and as the parents leave, the humanoid face appears in the window once more. Its teeth gnashing and its long fingernails

scrape against the window, already tasting the blood morsel it can't yet get to.

928. Deep in the Old West a group of cattle rustlers steal cows from what they think is a small, feeble bodied community. However, not only have they just stolen from vampires, but they've stolen the source of food that allowed them to resist hunting humans.

929. An unnamed character is rushed into the emergency room after being discovered half-starving on the side of the road. They are immediately put on nourishing fluids, but these don't seem to help. That's because they need fresh blood.

930. Most legends agree that when an individual becomes a vampire they must suffer a physical death first. Craft a scenario which focusses on the character's passing. End the scene with them awakening as a vampire.

931. For years an unnamed character has been picked on and bullied at school. As a result, when they turn, after attending a party for the first time, they immediately seek revenge.

932. Emotional, or psychic vampires do not live off blood, but rather the energy of others. Suppose an unnamed

character is such a creature and must drain someone completely before they are exposed.

933.   Using the concept of emotional vampires again suppose one has attacked the wrong character. This unnamed character is mentally unhinged and the vampire simply cannot handle this psychic overload.

934.   While walking home an unnamed character takes a detour, right through the town's cemetery. No, they don't come across a hungry vampire. Instead they come across the bodies of its victims.

935.   A vampire is caught nibbling on the neck of a human. If this wasn't bad enough, suppose they are caught by someone they care about. One who had no idea.

936.   Modern technology has made being a vampire easier. Now creatures of the night post online in order to find a willing victim. Often those who have nothing else to live for.

937.   A vampire travels from city-to-city all across the globe in order to try "cuisine" from different cultures. They meet their match in a young child in a remote mountain village.

938. An unnamed character is found buried in the snow, barely alive. What their saviors don't realize is that this is a vampire who has been hungry for quite some time.

939. A scientist captures and sedates a vampire before performing exploratory surgery on them. The scientist wants to know how the whole live-off-blood-but-still-be-dead process works. Too bad anethesia doesn't work on vampires.

940. A vampire's greatest asset is their teeth. This is why when one is being tortured their fangs are the first to go. Their torturer doesn't seem to realize that, while this is their greatest asset, it is not the vampire's only one.

941. A group of vampire hunters are breaking open caskets in order to locate the monster that's been feeding on the town's children. Little do they know the vampire is actually amongst them.

942. In the Old South, a vampire comes across a slave in the dead of night. After a brief tussle the slave bests the vampire. In exchange the vampire offers the slave freedom, by way of eternal life.

943. Vampires are often depicted as having long fangs while their other teeth remain relatively normal. Perhaps a

more horrifying scenario would be a vampire who only has row after row of razor sharp canines.

944. Suppose a vampire is a glutton, consuming blood more than they really should. As a result, this vampire is a bloated, walking blood sack.

945. An unnamed character wakes up to the sound of scratching at the window. When the character goes to investigate something large and heavy breaks through.

946. A group of vampires have managed to keep themselves from killing humans – by keeping one alive as an unwilling blood donor. Craft a narrative from the perspective of this unusual victim.

947. A vampire does not want to be a creature of the night. They attempt suicide only to discover that they cannot die by their own hand. In fact, they only become more powerful.

948. After living for centuries a vampire is rather bored of undead life. Perhaps a new type of prey will help stimulate them?

949. An unnamed character has been feeling rather sluggish lately. They even fall asleep at their desk. What they don't

know is that they are in the process of dying. Albeit slower than normally. Soon they will awaken as a vampire.

950.   An unnamed character narrowly misses another car by swerving off the side of the road. The car flips over a few times before crashing into a ditch. It is now a mangled mess and the character inside is bleeding profusely. They will certainly perish from their injuries, unless the vampire that appears shows mercy.

951.   Suppose that a child has been turned into a vampire. Unlike most children, when they have a temper tantrum, it can be downright deadly.

952.   An unnamed character is driving down a dark and desolate road in the dead of night. They have a strange feeling that something is amiss. Their instincts are spot on. There is a vampire on the roof of the car, waiting hungrily for it to stop.

953.   After waking up in the middle of the night an unnamed character wakes up to find a shadow standing over the bed. The character reaches for the gun hidden underneath the frame, but it's too late. The vampire is already at their throat.

954. One might be familiar with Elizabeth Bathory, the Hungarian Countess who lived during the 16th century. She was known for bathing in the blood of her victims in a vain attempt to stay beautiful forever. Suppose she truly was a vampire and an unnamed character is set to be her next victim.

955. Looking again at history, suppose an unnamed character is a solider in a large army, known far and wide for its brutality. That might have something to do with the fact that they are under the leadership of the famed vampire, Vlad the Impaler.

956. While sucking the blood of an unwilling victim a vampire suddenly pulls out in disgust. The victim laughs at the vampire's suffering, aware of the poison that is currently coursing through their veins.

957. In Chinese culture, vampires are known as *ch'iang shih* and have long, hook claws and bright red eyes. Suppose a group of them are now headed to a small village.

958. In some cultures becoming a vampire is directly caused by an improper burial. Envision a scenario in which an unnamed character is a grave keep who has been preventing the undead from rising for over fifty years. When they pass all of that will change.

959. Can animals be vampires? One small town is about to find out. Even pets suddenly begin to turn against their owners in an effort to satiate their new cravings.

960. An unnamed character is aware of their friend visiting the grave of a recently departed loved one every night. The character believes their friend is simply distraught. The truth is, they are feeding a newly awakened vampire.

961. An infection spreads across a small community. At first bad hygiene, like improper hand washing, is blamed. However, much like mosquitos and the West Nile Virus, it's actually vampires helping to spread the disease.

962. A church sees a large influx of bats in its bell tower. Priests believe an easy fix is to contact animal control. That won't work, because a battle between light and dark will soon be underway.

963. A vampire and a human have been friends for over 90 years. The vampire might have even knew the human before they turned. When it's the human's time to go, the vampire takes matters into their own undead hands. A decision they both will come to regret.

Other Beings

Although vampires, witches, and werewolves are the most common supernatural beings, there are certainly others. A host of other humanoid entities across cultures all fit very nicely in the horror genre. Again, the focus should always be on what kind of unique fear they may instill in unsuspecting victims rather than turning them into a cheesy plot device. Keep in mind that some of these creatures may have sprung up in a previous section. In the following narratives the focus should be on them and their otherness rather than outside themes.

964. The writer typed and something on the window knocked. The writer stopped and no sound could be heard. They typed again, and the sound would pick up again. Typing, knocking, typing, knocking, so on and so forth. Finally, the writer got up and looked out the window, expecting to find a sinister face staring back at them. After all, they did have quite the imagination. Little did they know – the strange humanoid creature was already in the room.

965. A supernatural being has been following an unnamed character for quite some time. The character has been completely oblivious to it, until they get into a car accident. Then they can see the entity hovering over them, staring down with a sinister smile.

966. Horror monsters are often used as a reflection of our darkest fears, whether they are clowns to represent innocence lost or demons to showcase questions of morality and religion. Craft your own unique monster and determine what primal fear it actually represents.

967. Similarly, craft a new twist on the idea of a strange being, rather than crafting a narrative where this creature hounds and harasses a mortal, instead write the piece from the monster's perspective.

968. An arson investigation is underway and firemen are helping to clean up the wreckage. "Over here!" They yell. It appears a few bodies have been found in the recovery. At least these *look* like charred human remains. On closer inspection its discovered that they aren't human at all.

969. An unnamed character is on vacation and has finally set up their tent in a forest retreat. They are happily relaxing by the fire until they see a strange humanoid figure watching them in the distance. Behind them, their tent begins to rustle.

970. Deep in the ruins of an old abandoned theme park, an urban explorer hears the distant sound of carnival music. That's when the giggling starts and something emerges from the shadows.

971. While at the circus, an unnamed character sneaks backstage to check out the animals up close and personal. Soon they find themselves surrounded by angry clowns. One in particular looks *quite* unusual.

972. An unnamed character has been given a small clown doll by an elderly grandparent. They only put it out when their relative comes to visit. The clown doesn't like that. Not one bit.

973. Camera at the ready, an animal photographer points at the murky swamp, waiting for an alligator to emerge. However, what comes out isn't an alligator at all, but rather a strange humanoid figure covered in scales.

974. After driving across country on a road trip an unnamed character finally makes it back home with a bounty of unusual gifts for their loved ones. Unbeknownst to them something else has come along for the ride.

975. An unnamed character is spending the night at a friend's house for the first time since their friendship began. The character agrees to sleep on the couch despite being creeped out by the enormous porcelain doll collection in the living room. In the middle of the night they wake up to the sound of several tiny footsteps.

976.   Generally it's creepy dolls that make it into the horror narrative. Try something different. Use action figures, stuffed animals, or another type of children's toy.

977.   It's the middle of a thunderstorm and an unnamed character is warm in bed, enjoying hot chocolate and a good book. Outside a figure is approaching the house, lightening illuminating its form every so often.

978.   A sailor is on a small boat after the ship they were on capsizes. They have no idea what happened to the rest of the crew, but are thankful to be alive themselves. In the distance they see a beautiful figure calling to them. They don't seem to notice the bones scattered around the rocks upon which they sit.

979.   An unnamed character is on a cruise ship when they decide to look for dolphins. Instead they see hundreds of humanoid creatures below the surface of the water.

980.   A family is having a heated argument over something trivial. This is not the first time this has happened. However, this *is* the first time a dark humanoid figure has been sent to teach them a lesson.

981. A young character hears the sound of an ice cream truck and hurriedly races to it. When they arrive, they find that none of the pictures on the side of the truck look like any treat they've ever seen before. They look like sigils of some sort. The driver also looks unusual, as they lean out the window, their head and neck extracting out, but nothing else.

982. An unnamed character makes the world's most wonderful compositions. Their music could even quiet the most terrifying beast. Instead it has the power to do the opposite. Strange and unusual beings are often drawn to these melodies.

983. The lights flicker on and off for a short time before the power cuts out completely. An unnamed character opens the breaker box to find several humanoid creatures tearing up the wires.

984. An unnamed character wakes up in excruciating pain. Below the covers one of their limbs has been removed and several creatures are carrying it back to their nest.

985. A morgue attendant is busy embalming a body, when they hear knocking coming from inside one of the storage units. They assume it's a prank and swing the drawer

open, hoping to catch the prankster in action. Instead they come across a humanoid creature feeding on a corpse.

986. There are many different types of cryptids all over the world. Take two of your favorite and mix them together to craft this narrative.

987. An unnamed character is scrolling through various blogs, searching for some creepy stories. They have no idea that while they are reading the horror tales of others, they are about to be in a scary tale of their own. Something is in the room watching them.

988. Creation stories are very common across many world religions. Take one such myth and add a secondary intelligent species aside from humankind. Perhaps this species is the prototype. Or we are.

989. One foggy morning while on the way home an unnamed character slams on their breaks on a desolate road. Laying before them is a humanoid creature unlike anything they've ever seen before.

990. Laughter and chatter suddenly dies down inside a tent when everyone is shushed by one of the characters. That's when the rest of the group sees it. The silhouette of

someone passing just outside. However, the figure is much too large to be human.

991.   An unnamed character has a one night stand after picking up a stranger in a bar. After the act is complete they feel funny and begin to trip over themselves. The last thing they see before they lose consciousness is their partner's skin coming off in clumps.

992.   An unnamed character is taking a leisurely stroll around the neighbourhood when they see a small child crouched and crying on the sidewalk. When they approach, the child suddenly snarls and jumps to its fully height, growing larger and larger.

993.   A group of friends are drinking and having a great time together. Their laughter is suddenly cut off by the sound of screeching. They follow the noise to the kitchen only to find a creature writhing on the ground, several bottles of alcohol empty around them.

994.   While enjoying a hot cup of coffee on their balcony an unnamed character suddenly sees something furry pass by. Upon closer inspection they can see that it is the head of a large humanoid figure.

995. A group of explorers are looking for a good camping spot on the side of the mountain where they are. They find a nice cave, which would do well to block out the winds, only it is already occupied. Inside a white humanoid figure is busy eating the remains of another travelling party.

996. An unnamed character hears the distant sound of singing from a meadow near their home. The sound is so beautiful that they decide to check it out. When they reach the source they come across dozens of humans no larger than a ruler. They aren't happy about being discovered and immediately attack.

997. An unnamed character barrels through the door and yells for their roommate to follow them outside. They are in such a panic that the roommate wastes no time. Outside the character shows them their damaged car, and the strange humanoid creature stuck in the windshield.

998. An unnamed character was supposed to pick up their new glasses weeks ago. They will soon regret it greatly. They come across a dog and reach out to pet it, only to realize too late that it isn't a dog at all.

999. A series of knocks rouses an unnamed character from their nap. They are a little annoyed, but answer the door

anyway. Before them are three children with snow white skin and dark black orbs for eyes.

1000. An experienced hiker hits their favorite trail for a late night adventure. Usually they can see owls with their prey or interesting spiders making new homes. This time their light shines on a four foot tall humanoid hanging from the trees.

1001. A rancher notices that several of their pigs have gone missing. There's no hole in the fence and no other way they could have gotten out. They decide to set up a camera to see if it happens again. Nothing could prepare them to the sight of a humanoid creature with wings sweeping down and carrying off a small, squealing body.

ABOUT THE AUTHOR

Christina Escamilla is a horror author that loves diving straight into psychologically haunting themes. When she isn't disturbing the masses, she can be seen exploring obscure local spots, communing with nature, or adding more strangeness to her ever growing oddity collection.

To learn more about her visit: www.stinaesc.com

Made in the USA
Coppell, TX
27 April 2025

48750422R00156